THE ASSYRIANS

LOST CIVILIZATIONS

The books in this series explore the rise and fall of the great civilizations and peoples of the ancient world. Each book considers not only their history but their art, culture and lasting legacy and asks why they remain important and relevant in our world today.

Already published:

The Assyrians Paul Collins
The Aztecs Frances F. Berdan
The Barbarians Peter Bogucki
Egypt Christina Riggs
The Etruscans Lucy Shipley
The Goths David M. Gwynn
The Greeks Philip Matyszak
The Hittites Damien Stone
The Inca Kevin Lane
The Indus Andrew Robinson
The Maya Megan E. O'Neil
Nubia Sarah M. Schellinger
The Persians Geoffrey Parker and Brenda Parker
The Phoenicians Vadim S. Jigoulov
The Sumerians Paul Collins
The Three Kingdoms of Korea Richard D. McBride II

THE ASSYRIANS
LOST CIVILIZATIONS

PAUL COLLINS

REAKTION BOOKS

For Thomas and Katie

Published by Reaktion Books Ltd
Unit 32, Waterside
44–48 Wharf Road
London N1 7UX, UK

www.reaktionbooks.co.uk

First published 2024

Printed and bound in India by Replika Press Pvt. Ltd

A catalogue record for this book is available from the British Library

ISBN 978 1 78914 923 4

CONTENTS

Chronology

c. 6000–5000 BC	Halaf period. Village at Nineveh
c. 5000–4000 BC	Late Ubaid period
c. 4000–3100 BC	Uruk period
c. 3100–2600 BC	Ninevite V period in north Mesopotamia; Jemdet Nasr and Early Dynastic periods in south Mesopotamia
c. 2800 BC	Ashur settled
c. 2350–2150 BC	Agade Empire
c. 2100–2000 BC	Third Dynasty of Ur
c. 1960–1840 BC	Karum Kanesh flourishing
c. 1810–1750 BC	Kingdom of Samsi-Addu
c. 1500–1250 BC	Mittanian kingdom
1356–1150 BC	Middle Assyrian kingdom. Assur-uballit I is first king of Assyria. Shalmaneser I defeats Mittani. Tukulti-Ninurta I builds new royal

	centre and captures Babylon. Tiglath-pileser I faces Aramaean migrations
883–612 BC	Neo-Assyrian Empire. Assurnasirpal II founds Kalhu (Nimrud). Tiglath-pileser III conquers new territory, establishes provinces. Sargon II founds Dur-Sharrukin (Khorsabad). Sennacherib establishes Nineveh as capital. Esarhaddon invades Egypt. Civil war between Assurbanipal and Shamash-shumu-ukin
614 BC	Destruction of Assur temple
612 BC	Fall of Nineveh
605–539 BC	Neo-Babylonian Empire
539–331 BC	Achaemenid Persian Empire. Cult of Assur restored at Ashur
331–141 BC	Seleucid Empire
141 BC–AD 224	Parthian Empire. New temple of Assur built
224–641	Sasanian Empire. Ashur destroyed. Arbela (Erbil) and Nineveh become centres of Christianity
641–61	Rashidun Caliphate
661–750	Umayyad Caliphate
750–1258	Abbasid Caliphate
1258	Mongol forces capture and sack Baghdad
1508–1638	Safavid Persian Empire

1638–1918	Ottoman Empire
1800–1914	European exploration and excavation of Assyrian sites, and finds removed to London, Paris, Berlin and Constantinople (Istanbul)
1914	British invasion and occupation of Mesopotamia
1921	Kingdom of Iraq established
1922–74	European and American excavations, division of finds between Iraq and excavators
1926	Baghdad Antiquities Museum opens
1932	Britain declares Iraq independent
1966	Iraq Museum in Baghdad opens
1972	Enlarged Mosul Museum opens
1990–91	Gulf War, Mosul Museum looted
2003	U.S.-led invasion of Iraq. Iraq Museum and Mosul Museum looted
2014–17	Iraqi Civil War; defeat of ISIS/Da'esh
	Destruction of Mosul Museum, extensive damage to Assyrian sites
2022	Iraq Museum reopens

Arabs and Nestorians moving a slab at Kouyunjik (Nineveh), 1853.

ONE

Ancient and Modern Empires

Five men stand in a row, shoulder to shoulder, leaning back to take the weight of an enormous stone panel that a sixth man struggles to control with a rope as it is lowered from the front of a mud-brick wall. The men are distinguished by their headgear: Arabs wear turbans, while the three men in pointed felt hats can be identified as Nestorian Christians, although it is possible that they thought of themselves as Assyrians. The irony of the scene – an engraving from an English book published in 1853, three years after the event depicted[1] – is that these men are helping to dismantle the remains of an ancient Assyrian royal palace, and thus part of their own heritage, in order for the sculpted slab to be removed to London (a story to which we will very shortly return).

The idea that there might be people who identified themselves as Assyrians living in eastern Turkey and northern Iraq, then part of the vast Ottoman Empire, would be a source of surprise to Western travellers only a decade before the stone relief was uncovered and taken away. In May 1841, for example, the Reverend Horatio Southgate, a Protestant clergyman from the United States, arrived at the village of Harput (Kharberd) in eastern Turkey and stopped with his companions for breakfast.[2] He was at the start a journey of several months with the aim of learning about the condition of Christians in this part of the predominantly Muslim empire. Of particular interest were people commonly known at the time as Nestorians, Jacobites or Syrian Jacobites. In an account of his travels Southgate recalls,

> I began to make inquiries for the Syrians. The people informed me there that were about one hundred families of them in the town of Kharpout, a village inhabited by them on the plain. I observed that the Armenians did not know them under the name which I used, *Syriani*; but called them ASSOURI, which struck me the more at the moment from its resemblance to our English name Assyrians, from whom they claim their origin, being sons, as they say, of Assour (Asshur) who 'out of the land of Shinar went forth, and builded Nineveh, and the city Rehoboth, and Calah, and Resin between Nineveh and Calah: the same is a great city.' (Genesis 10:11–12)[3]

Here were people who offered a connection to the Hebrew Bible with its descriptions of a mighty Assyrian Empire, including the names of some of its kings: Tiglath-pileser, Sargon, Sennacherib and Esarhaddon, and their capital cities of Calah and Nineveh. Given that knowledge of the Bible was considered a fundamental aspect of a Christian education during the nineteenth century, the Assyrians would have been very familiar to many people, even to children who had only attended a Sunday school. Those who could afford a private education or a fee-charging school were also expected to acquire a knowledge of the surviving works of ancient Greek and Roman authors, some of which contain accounts of the so-called Orient (essentially the lands of North Africa and those to the east of the Mediterranean Sea), with references to some of its peoples, including the Assyrians. In this way pupils came to know the works of the later fifth-century BC Greek historian Herodotus, who describes Assyria as the first empire to rule over western Asia, as well as quotations from Ctesias of Cnidus (writing around 390 BC), with his accounts of Queen Semiramis and the kings Ninus and Sardanapalus, who are presented as either astonishing individuals or worthy of condemnation for their excessive sexuality and self-indulgence.

Such captivating narratives became a source of inspiration for artists and writers, and this was especially the case with the Romantic movement of the late eighteenth and early nineteenth centuries. One poet in particular has probably done more than any other to shape the Western reception of Assyria: Lord Byron (1788–1824). In 1815, at the height of his fame in Regency London, Byron wrote the Hebrew Melodies, thirty poems intended to be a choral work, which included 'The Destruction of Sennacherib'. Based on the biblical account of the Assyrian siege of Jerusalem (2 Kings 18–19, Isaiah 36–7), the poem's most famous lines are those of its first stanza:

> The Assyrian came down like the wolf on the fold,
> And his cohorts were gleaming in purple and gold;
> And the sheen of their spears was like stars on the sea,
> When the blue wave rolls nightly on deep Galilee.

In 1821 Byron returned to the theme of Assyria but on this occasion relied on the classical sources to write a historical tragedy in blank verse. Titled *Sardanapalus*, it describes the fall of the ancient empire and its last king, who commits suicide rather than surrendering to invaders. The play inspired the French painter Eugène Delacroix (1798–1863) to produce one of the most powerful yet shocking visual imaginings of Assyria. The enormous painting (some 4 by 5 metres), now in the Louvre Museum, depicts the moment when Sardanapalus decides to kill himself, but Delacroix transforms the scene into a violent sexual fantasy in which the hedonistic monarch watches disinterestedly after giving the order that all his favourite possessions – including his female attendants and horses – should be destroyed.

In Western culture, therefore, Assyria had come to be imagined as the fusion of an exotic and erotic caricature of the Turkish Ottoman royal court with thundering stories of biblical oppression. There seemed little question, however, that the empire had been a historical reality, not least since echoes of it existed beyond the evidence provided by classical and Old Testament authors. These faint reverberations could be found in its ancient heartland of northern Iraq, where the abandoned remains of settlements sometimes retained their ancient names and, as we will explore towards the end of this book, folk tales about Assyrian kings and officials circulated in local languages. Indeed, a number of Arab and Persian scholars

Eugène Delacroix, *The Death of Sardanapalus*, 1827, oil on canvas.

refer to such sites in their writings as early as the tenth century. The Arab geographer Yakut al-Hamawi, for example, records in his renowned *Mu'jam ul-Buldan* (Dictionary of Countries), written between 1224 and 1228, that the village of Khorsabad was on the site of an Assyrian city called Saraoun or Saraghoun, where 'considerable treasures were found amongst the ruins'.[4] This is the Assyrian capital Dur-Sharrukin. Other sites are described in the accounts of travellers, such as Rabbi Benjamin of Tudela (1130–1173):

> Thence it is two days to Mosul, which is Assur the Great, and here dwell about 7,000 Jews . . . Mosul is the frontier town of the land of Persia. It is a very large and ancient city, situated on the river Hiddekel [Tigris], and is connected with Nineveh by means of a bridge. Nineveh is in ruins, but amid the ruins there are villages and hamlets, and the extent of the city may be determined by the walls, which extend forty parasangs [approximately 220 km (137 mi.)] to the city of Irbil.[5]

So, when European merchants, soldiers and officials with antiquarian interests arrived in this part of the Ottoman Empire, they had much historical and local knowledge to draw on. The numbers of such individuals began to increase following Napoleon Bonaparte's invasion of Egypt in 1798, which resulted in the appearance of the French Navy in the Indian Ocean and the Persian Gulf. The British had already established a toehold in the region in the shape of the British East India Company, which had founded a trading post or 'factory' in the port of Basra as early as 1641. By the late eighteenth century, the region called, in Arabic, 'Iraq' (and known in the West as Mesopotamia) had become a strategic overland route between the Mediterranean and the Indian subcontinent, where the Company's private army was violently establishing its control. As a result, a British political agent was appointed in Baghdad, and this was soon followed by the opening of a British consulate in the city.

In early 1808 a young man of 21 named Claudius James Rich arrived in Baghdad with his wife Mary to take up the political post of East India Company Resident. He was a brilliant linguist, becoming fluent in Arabic, Persian and Turkish and with more than a passing knowledge of French, Greek, Latin, Hebrew, Syriac and Mandarin Chinese. Rich also had antiquarian interests, and during his time in Mesopotamia he carried out investigations into a number of ancient sites, including mapping the walls of the ruins understood to be those of Nineveh and examining the remains at a place called Nimrud, learning from the inhabitants of surrounding villages that these were the remains of cities associated with Al Athur or Ashur.[6] As he explored the ruins, he collected a number of bricks with wedge-shaped or cuneiform inscriptions of a type that scholars back in Europe were struggling to decipher; following the death of her husband in 1821, Mary sold these to the British Museum, thereby establishing the foundations of its Assyrian collections.[7]

It was, however, a representative of France who would initiate more substantial archaeological work. This began in late 1842, when the French consul at Mosul, Paul-Émile Botta, had local men dig trenches in the large settlement mound known as Kouyunjik, part of ancient Nineveh, where gossip spoke of buried stone sculptures. The results were, however, disappointing; just fragments of inscribed gypsum and brick. After a few months into this work, however, Botta was informed by a man from the village of Khorsabad, about 15 kilometres (9 mi.) to the northeast of Mosul, that impressive monuments had recently been found when his neighbours had dug foundations for new houses. Botta despatched some men to investigate and, with the account confirmed, he shifted his workers to Khorsabad and had a wide trench opened. The villagers imagined that he must be searching for more of the treasure that Yakut al-Hamawi had described. As the accumulated soil was removed it became apparent that a large room was being revealed formed from mud-brick walls lined with huge slabs of gypsum covered with extraordinary carved scenes of battles, sieges and banquets.

The news of Botta's finds caused considerable excitement in Europe. Here was evidence in stone of the Assyrian Empire. The discovery encouraged the French government to provide Botta with funds to undertake significantly larger excavations at Khorsabad. When these were concluded in 1845, Botta selected the best-preserved sculptures and, with the permission of the Ottoman authorities, had them packed into crates, hauled to the Tigris, floated on rafts south to Basra and shipped to France and the Louvre Museum in Paris.[8] The majority of the reliefs uncovered at the site were, however, left *in situ* either because they were too fragile to move or because their imagery was considered similar to sculptures bound for France.

Among those who recognized the significance of these discoveries was an Englishman, Austen Henry Layard (1817–1894). He was an acquaintance of Botta's who by 1843 was working in Constantinople as both an agent for the British embassy and a foreign correspondent; he wrote excitedly about the French achievements in the *Malta Times* and his reports were reproduced in a number of European journals. Layard's enthusiasm for Botta's excavations was shared by his friend Alexander Hector (1810–1875), who had settled in Baghdad as a merchant. Following Botta's departure for France, Hector visited, perhaps on more than one occasion, the now abandoned trenches at Khorsabad and removed reliefs from various areas of the palace.[9] Because of the scale of the sculptures (complete stone panels could measure some 3 by 2.5 metres (10 by 8 ft) and weigh several tons), only sections of the reliefs – generally the heads of humans and horses, as well as inscriptions – were removed, sawn from the larger figures to make them manageable for transport. With their size reduced, Hector's carvings did not need to follow the route taken by Botta's complete reliefs but rather travelled westward from Mosul by camel caravan to the port of Iskenderun on the Mediterranean.

Hector may have realized that there would likely be a potential market for the reliefs given the immense excitement in England aroused by the Khorsabad discoveries; he would later sell fifty of his fragments to the British Museum.[10] However, the sculptures had also come to play a role in the imperialist rivalry being played out between France and Britain in the Middle East. Hector's motives for removing reliefs could thus be interpreted by some in Britain as 'a patriotic desire to secure to the nation any relics or information of value'.[11] Indeed, the need to confront the French success induced Sir Stratford Canning, the British ambassador in Constantinople (modern Istanbul), to sponsor excavations by Henry Layard at Nimrud, where discoveries, the ambassador hoped, would 'beat the Louvre hollow'.[12]

In this atmosphere of nationalistic competition, four of the Khorsabad sculptures, almost certainly part of the collection gathered by Hector, were forwarded to Canning. Although not impressed by the artistic value of the sculptures, he was keen to promote a personal connection with the excavations and thus curry favour with two of the most powerful British politicians of the day: the Marquess of Lansdowne and the British prime minister, Sir Robert Peel. Each man was therefore sent two reliefs.[13] One of the Lansdowne reliefs depicts the head of a beardless Assyrian attendant, facing left. This man has typical wavy hair which is brushed behind his ears and ends in rows of tight curls at the shoulder. He wears a large three-armed earring and his fringed garment is ornamented at the shoulder with two bands of alternating rosettes and concentric squares, presumably intended to represent embroidery. The sculpture was possibly cut from carved panels that depict a procession

Head of beardless attendant, Dur-Sharrukin (Khorsabad), *c.* 710 BC.

approaching the king in which attendants carry vessels and furniture in preparation for a celebratory banquet.

By the beginning of January 1846 the reliefs had arrived at Whitehall, the centre of government in London. They were the first such reliefs to reach Europe; Botta's sculptures arrived in France towards the end of that year. By that time, however, Layard's workmen had been uncovering inscribed stone panels and sculpted slabs from a number of palace buildings at Nimrud as well as at Nineveh, where he had trenches opened. The significance of the finds encouraged the British government to take over the financing of the excavations through the British Museum; the first relief panels from Nimrud arrived in London in 1847.

Although the excavators recorded their debt to local knowledge, the European press and other writers depicted Botta and Layard as 'discovering' Assyria – something that has successfully entered much of the literature. Long associated with biblical oppression, Assyria now became associated with the 'heroic' uncovering of their royal palaces and the transport of the colossal sculptures across the globe. As such, the ancient monuments were also linked with Victorian enterprise and science, so, for example, King Sennacherib, who established Nineveh as the Assyrian capital around 700 BC, is depicted on the Albert Memorial (unveiled in 1872) in London's Kensington Gardens as the embodiment of engineering. In parallel, scholars sought to fit the Assyrian reliefs into the established art-historical canon. The sculptures came to be viewed as a link in a developmental sequence that led from the achievements of Egyptian art to the idealized humanism of ancient Greece, being perceived as an art of power, grandeur and violence in contrast to Egyptian calm and Greek beauty.[14]

The excavation of the Assyrian royal palaces had revealed not only stone carvings, but fragments of wall paintings, glazed bricks and extraordinary objects in metal, ivory and glass. In addition, tens of thousands of clay tablets impressed with the same cuneiform writing as carved across many of the reliefs were uncovered and transferred to London. By 1850 significant progress had been made in translating these texts and it was apparent that the vast majority of inscriptions recorded a Semitic language related to modern

Detail of the Albert Memorial, London, showing King Sennacherib among the Great Engineers of the Ancient World.

Arabic and Hebrew; named Akkadian, it had recognizable Assyrian and Babylonian dialects.

Collections of Assyrian objects also came to be displayed in the capitals of other imperial powers beyond Britain and France: an archaeological museum was founded in Constantinople as early as 1869, the same year an Ottoman law was introduced to regulate excavation and the ownership of finds; and the Pergamon Museum in Berlin began to be constructed in 1906 to house material being excavated by German archaeologists at the site of Ashur – the building would be completed in 1930. By that later date the Oriental Institute of the University of Chicago had added a new gallery to its museum for the display of sculptures shipped to the United States from the excavations it had sponsored at Khorsabad, while the Metropolitan Museum of Art, New York, had started to plan the installation of Assyrian reliefs from Nimrud that had been gifted to them by John D. Rockefeller Jr.[15] Other institutions acquired examples of sculptures, seals and tablets from individuals who had plundered them from sites in Iraq or purchased them through antiquities dealers. Assyria thus came to play a recognizable role in the historical narratives of civilization as presented in museums around the world as well as in written accounts. This was also true in Iraq itself, where, under British occupation in the aftermath of the First World War, the Baghdad Antiquities Museum (later the Iraq Museum) was established in 1926 and where Assyrian monuments and objects came to be shown alongside those of ancient Sumer and Babylonia as symbols of national identity.

Few modern visitors to these museums who stand before the Assyrian reliefs can fail to be awed by both their scale and the images carved across them. Until relatively recently, it was often taken for granted that the scenes of hunting, battle and siege were the products of a violent and cruel society. But is this interpretation correct? The question can now be answered with some confidence as over the last few decades an astonishingly detailed picture of Assyria has been reconstructed from archaeology, ancient texts and images. The evidence is immensely rich and there are therefore many ways in which Assyria's history and culture can be explored. This book reveals Assyria through the lens of some its greatest buildings, literature, learning and art, much of which was inevitably commissioned by the most powerful people in Assyrian society: the royal family, the nobility and wealthy individuals. While the following pages therefore tell less about the ordinary person in the streets of Nimrud, Dur-Sharrukin and Nineveh, they offer an insight into the world of Assyria that readers are most likely to encounter as visitors to museums and as local, regional and international tourists exploring the ancient Assyrian sites in Iraq itself.

Painted Halaf-style bowl, Arpachiyah, Iraq, *c.* 5500 BC.

TWO
Ancient Origins

A modern traveller following the river Tigris north from Baghdad leaves behind the flat and fertile alluvial plains of southern Iraq (ancient Babylonia) with its irrigation channels and canals and once-extensive date groves and marshlands. Gradually the vegetation thins into an arid region of steppe until, after some 250 kilometres (155 mi.), the landscape dramatically and abruptly changes with the appearance of a jagged mountain range stretching across our wanderer's path. These are the Hamrin Mountains that form a natural boundary between Babylonia and the world of Assyria. Breached by the Tigris, the peaks, some up to 300 metres (1,000 ft), taper off to the north into chains of rocky outcrops. One of these forms a 25-metre-high (82 ft) vertical cliff around which the Tigris makes a sharp bend. Here, at the top of the escarpment and overlooking the river, at a site now known as Qa'lat Sherqat, lay the city of Ashur, the place that would give its name to Assyrian culture.[1]

Ashur was located at the border between the dry steppe where pastoralists moved with flocks of sheep, and the heartland of Assyria to the north and east, a region of good soils and rain-fed agriculture that can produce large-scale harvests of wheat and barley. Passing along the river for a further 60 kilometres (37 mi.) brings our traveller to the confluence of the Tigris and the Great Zab, a major tributary flowing from the east and one of several routes across the heartland towards the Zagros Mountains and the rich agricultural plains around the city of Erbil (ancient Arbela). Pressing on north, however, takes the voyager past the remains of Nimrud (ancient

Kalhu, biblical Calah) before a further 30 kilometres (19 mi.) brings them to the city of Mosul and the ruins of what had been Assyria's greatest royal centre, Nineveh.

Drawing lines on a map to connect in turn Ashur, Nineveh and Arbela forms what has been described as the 'Assyrian triangle', with Kalhu at its centre.[2] The cities at the points of the triangle were all important centres for trade. Nineveh is located at a crossing of the Tigris and a natural stopping point on the overland route through Syria along the foothills of the Taurus Mountains towards the Mediterranean and into Anatolia. Similarly, Ashur dominated a ford of the river – although unlike Nineveh it lies on the western bank – with control of tracks leading across the steppe to the river Euphrates. In the east, Arbela is situated at the foothills of the Zagros Mountains, from where a number of roads lead to the resource-rich highlands of Iran.

Let us start our story long before Ashur and Assyria came into existence, since both the city and the civilization it produced are rooted in a region with a deep prehistory. This much is evident at Nineveh, which began as a village of mud-brick houses inhabited by families of farmers and herders sometime in the period from 6500 to 6000 BC. The small community was sustained by the very fertile and well-irrigated land at the confluence of the rivers Khosr and Tigris and its way of life was common to dozens of comparable settlements that dotted the Nineveh plain. It is very possible that Arbela also originated around this time but its very early history has yet to be investigated.

This was a world in which there were close connections between the scattered villages, sometimes over considerable distances. People herded their cattle and sheep to far-flung pastures as the seasons changed, and raw resources and finished goods, such as baskets, woven textiles and handmade pottery vessels and figurines, were exchanged between settlements. The most attractive products of these villagers were certainly bowls and plates produced in a very distinctive style, the finest examples of which are extremely thin-walled and exquisitely painted with delicate designs. This so-called Halaf pottery has been found from southeastern Turkey to Iran. It seems clear that there were specialized production centres for high-quality wares but also much regional copying, and it is possible that the vessels were being exchanged as prestige items between local elites. Some of the most beautifully painted of these polychrome ceramics were made around 5500 BC and come from the site of Arpachiyah, close to Nineveh. Despite its fragmentary nature and very faded black, white and red paint, one fine bowl hints at the glorious colour and decoration of such vessels. It is adorned at the centre of its interior with a sixteen-petalled rosette, perhaps a daisy, on a red ground and encircled by a chain of black dots and a wider band on which there are three rows of small black squares, each containing four white petals. A further chain of black dots on a buff ground is separated from the red edge of the bowl by four rows of dotted black circles. The meaning of the design, if its maker intended one, is unknown, but it could suggest a carpet of wild flowers of the sort that fill the landscape around Nineveh in spring. It is also possible that the rosette alludes to the supernatural world, a motif and idea to which we will return.

Over time a different style of pottery (Ubaid), one that had its origins in the communities of southern Mesopotamia, came to replace the Halaf ceramics, and with it came changes to some of the other distinctive attributes of people's lifestyles. The layout of rooms in homes, for example, became more standardized, presumably reflecting shared approaches to working and socializing.[3] There were also new designs carved on small pendants of stone. These may have originated as amulets, with the choice of stone and incised designs acting to protect the owner by connecting them with divine forces. By pressing the carved surface into a lump of clay covering the knot of a cord closing a container, the amulet could also serve to magically protect the contents from interference. Such seal impressions, however, also served as a mark of ownership and they became a means for managing transactions and the storage and distribution of resources as some villages expanded to become market towns and cities. Indeed, connections north and south along the foothills of the Zagros Mountains, as well as from east to west across the steppe, encouraged such developments as people travelled with their animals and exchanged products and ideas. A dramatic result was that between around 4200 and 3800 BC a number of small

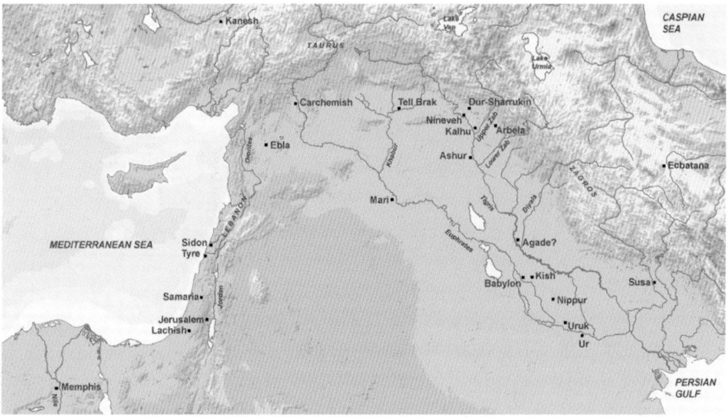

Map of the ancient Middle East with key sites.

sites were transformed into large urban centres; Nineveh was one of these.

The reasons for the growth of particular settlements towards a scale and organization that we can describe as a city are far from obvious, not least as this was the very first time anywhere on the planet that people came together to live in such close proximity in such large numbers. It is likely that it was in response to a combination of pressures – climatic, political, economic, perhaps even religious – that urban life became compelling; effectively, it came about as an attempt to confront the problem of periodic, unpredictable shortages and to enable concentration points for storage and distribution and for shared ideas. Over time – and this may have been across several centuries – Nineveh expanded by at least 40 hectares (100 ac), which might suggest a population of between 5,000 and 10,000 people.[4]

The developments at Nineveh are comparable with what was happening across the region at a number of other widely dispersed sites, including further east in a very fertile region of northern Syria at Tell Brak. As excavations here have focused on this very period, the findings offer clues to what may have been occurring at contemporary Nineveh. A number of villages close to Brak were abandoned, their populations perhaps emigrating (whether willingly or forcibly is unknown) to the growing town, where monumental mud-brick architecture was constructed. Alongside this urbanization came changes in the local economy, including specialization, with mass production concentrated at the edges of the site. Neighbouring communities appear to have delivered goods as tribute or tax to central institutions at Brak, where they were stored and redistributed. They arrived in containers closed with clay seal impressions and it may be significant that among the seal designs is one of a man spearing a lion, an image that would be closely associated with kingship in later periods.[5]

Such centres of trade and ritual were hubs in a network of relations that included cities on the Babylonian alluvium. From the middle of the fourth millennium BC, contact across Mesopotamia became much more integrated. People from the south, perhaps from places like Uruk, a vast urban centre at the head of the Persian Gulf, followed the routes along the Zagros foothills and the Euphrates valley into the rain-fed farming lands to the north. This contact can be recognized in the archaeological record by the presence of district Uruk-style pottery, architecture and seals, but it took different

Seal impression, Tell Brak, Syria, *c.* 3800–3600 BC.

forms depending on relationships established with the existing communities.[6] At some sites small colonies or enclaves were established within settlements but elsewhere it may have involved the takeover and occupation of entire sites. The newcomers engaged in acquiring and processing local products such as wool and flint, as well as metals, hard stones and strong wood not available at home, and probably exchanging them for other goods, including perhaps textiles imported from the south. There is no need to envisage this as a single planned, coordinated enterprise, but rather as much more piecemeal interaction with neighbouring regions that changed in form and intensity across several centuries. At Nineveh these relations are demonstrated by the excavation of seal impressions with designs used in south Mesopotamia, where cylinder seals were coming to replace stamps. In addition, a so-called numerical tablet has been uncovered. These are simple record-keeping tools comprising small tablets of clay that were impressed with signs representing numbers or quantities. By the later fourth millennium they formed part of much more complex administrative tools being developed at Uruk, which includes the precursors of writing.

Around 3100 BC, however, the colonies were being abandoned. Changes in rainfall patterns over a number of years appear to have led to drought and this had a profound impact on crop yields across northern Mesopotamia, forcing farmers to adopt different forms of subsistence, including turning to pastoralism. In parallel, or perhaps as a result of the deterioration in the climate, people in the surrounding highlands began to move in large numbers seeking more favourable places to settle. The previously integrated economies began to falter, leading to the emergence of small rural settlements at the expense of cities, which were abandoned or shrank in scale. A few places remained reasonably large, perhaps because they not only continued to act as market towns but were a focus for pilgrimage and worship in small temples. Nineveh had one such shrine where miniature jars, perhaps originally containing scented oils, were deposited. This temple was repeatedly rebuilt and later evidence indicates that it was dedicated to a great goddess who would play a central role in the story of Assyria. She was worshipped across the region in many manifestations and one of her later divine titles, Nin

(Sumerian for 'lady' and 'queen'), may even be present in the very name of Nineveh.[7] Aspects of her could be worshipped as the goddesses Ninlil and Inana, names that already appear in the late fourth millennium BC texts from Uruk.[8] The earliest surviving reference to the goddess at Nineveh (around 2050 BC) calls her Shaushka, another name for the more familiar Ishtar.[9]

If changes in the climate were responsible for transforming the settlement pattern across northern Mesopotamia, the same was also true to the south. The farmers of the Babylonian alluvium, however, were not dependent on rainfall for their crops as long as the multiple streams that crossed the region continued to flow and ditches could be dug to bring water to the fields of barley and plantations of date palms. Not only did cities continue to exist, but populations were increasingly concentrated within them. Networks of large settlements were linked by the river branches and shared a common culture in which scribes used the cuneiform script on clay to help manage workers, the storage and distribution of products and the transfer of property.

Commercial connections across Mesopotamia were maintained but now at a much less integrated level. At Nineveh the movement of resources took place without the need for writing, but seals continued to be employed for the purpose and these had designs similar to those in use along the Zagros foothills into southern Mesopotamia and southeast Iran. And, significantly, trade started to be funnelled through two newly established sites strategically located between the cities of the alluvium and the northern communities.

Around 2900 BC the city of Mari was founded a few kilometres from the river Euphrates in eastern Syria. It was a site ill-suited for agriculture and its distance from the river, probably in response to the threat posed by annual flooding, would have made it impractical as an emporium without the construction of a 2-kilometre (1 mi.) canal for boats. Yet the location of Mari gave it control over the Euphrates river traffic from northwestern Syria as well as that of the river Khabur from the east, thereby connecting the mineral-rich mountainous north and the cities of the south.[10]

The other foundation, and one fundamental for our story, was the city of Ashur. Like Mari, the new settlement was not located in a major agricultural area, but, as we have seen, occupied the top of an escarpment with steep sides facing the river Tigris to the north and east. This provided the settlement with natural protection, while the defence of its southern and western slopes would be achieved with walls and a moat. From their high vantage point, the inhabitants of Ashur could view both boat and foot traffic moving up and down the valley, as well as being well placed to control people and their flocks and herds making use of a ford to cross the river. It is far from clear when Ashur was first settled but there was almost certainly a community there by around 2700 BC.

The earliest building known at Ashur is a temple, although the name of its resident deity is uncertain. A much later temple at this location contained dedications to Ishtar and so it is possible that she had always been the focus of devotion.[11] There is, however, remarkable evidence for some of the rituals that took place in the building between around 2500 and 2400 BC, which included the practice of dedicating stone and inlaid statues of men and women. These are comparable in style with statues found in sanctuaries at Mari as well as at many other sites across the Babylonian alluvium, very clearly demonstrating a shared cultural world linked through trade and pilgrimage. It seems likely that these statues were thought to embody the very essence of worshippers so that their spirit would be present when the physical body was not. Unlike some sculptures found at other sites, the figures from Ashur are not inscribed with cuneiform, so we know nothing of the professions, let alone the names, of the people who dedicated them. It is possible that they were commissioned by individuals who undertook certain priestly duties or had sufficient status that allowed them access to the temple in this form. The statues may have been intended to ensure their continued participation in rituals, both inside the relatively small temple building and in its courtyard, where their statues could have received the offerings and prayers of worshippers on behalf of the god. The quality of carving of some of the sculptures is especially fine. Among them is a bearded man wearing only a tufted skirt, which may be sheepskin and intended to link him with the main sacrificial animal. His head and upper lip are shaved and the eye sockets and single line of his eyebrows would have originally

Votive limestone figure of a man, Ashur, *c.* 2500–2400 BC.

contained inlays of coloured stones. When complete, the figure would have stood over 50 centimetres (20 in.) high, and even in his damaged state the statue suggests an important individual in the life of the early city.

Although no written documents from this time have been uncovered at Ashur and Nineveh, cuneiform tablets have been discovered at Mari and, much further west, at Ebla. They record an early form of Akkadian and they depict a dynamic world of warfare and shifting alliances between city states in competition for land, water and trade; with an improvement of climatic conditions, urban life had returned to north Mesopotamia. At the heart of both Mari and Ebla lay a royal palace alongside temples of the gods who were thought to support the ruling king. These institutions employed many thousands of agricultural workers in the surrounding fields as well as for processing raw materials and manufacturing finished goods.

Further south, on the Babylonian plains, Kish may have been a dominant city, with perhaps another twenty or so city states dividing the alluvium between them. In the ancient cities at the head of the Persian Gulf, where Sumerian was the main written language, temples appear to have played a more significant political and economic role than palaces and at least some of the priestly rulers would be buried in splendour, as suggested by the famous Royal Graves at Ur, where the tombs included not only rich and exotic materials such as lapis lazuli and gold, but sacrificed human victims.

Around 2330 BC a man with links to Kish had gained sufficient followers that he was able to establish his own royal centre at Agade (Akkad), probably located around 80 kilometres (50 mi.) or so to the north. He adopted the Akkadian name Sargon (Sharru-ken), 'the king is legitimate', and by defeating a rival king, Lugalzagesi, who had himself defeated a series of city state rulers, he was able to claim supremacy over Babylonia. His two sons and grandson, Rimush, Manishtushu and Naram-Sin, who succeeded him in succession between about 2280 and 2220 BC, extended their influence and wealth with raids to western Iran and northern Syria, including sacking Mari and Ebla and establishing a strategic base at Nagar (Tell Brak).

It is possible that Ashur enjoyed a degree of independence from Agade. An inscribed alabaster plaque was dedicated in this period to the goddess Ishtar by a certain Ititi, who is called 'overseer'.[12] Whether he was the local ruler or an appointee of the Agade kings is unclear but either way he attempted to extend his influence over neighbouring towns since the inscription claims the plaque was part of the booty from Gasur (the town of Nuzi – modern Yorgan Tepe – to the east of Ashur). That there were at least periods when Ashur fell within the orbit of Agade is suggested by an inscribed bronze spearpoint, also from the Ishtar temple, that was dedicated by a man called Azuzu who calls himself the 'servant' of Manishtushu.[13] The rulers of Agade themselves make no reference to Ashur or Nineveh in their inscriptions, though later traditions claimed that Manishtushu constructed a temple for Ishtar at Nineveh.

The Agade kings faced repeated rebellions, both in the Babylonian heartland of their empire and also at the fringes. By around 2150 BC, perhaps exacerbated by another extended period of drought, the empire had rapidly collapsed. In what is likely to have been a time of disorder and confusion, it was also a moment to wreak revenge by attacking the monuments of rulers whose power had been maintained by brute force. It may, therefore, have been at this time that an almost life-size statue of an Agade king was targeted for destruction with calculated precision.[14] All that remains today is the 35-centimetre-high (13 in.) copper alloy head, separated at the neck from what may have been a full-scale standing or seated figure. Found at Nineveh, it is the product of a court art of remarkable refinement and naturalism that emerged under Manishtushu and Naram-Sin. The head was made using the lost-wax method, an extraordinary technological accomplishment for such an impressive large-scale sculpture in the round. The monarch's face conveys a calm majesty; a portrait of kingship rather than of a specific ruler. The heavy, patterned and carefully modelled beard contrasts with the smooth surface of the face and the finely modelled lips. An elaborately plaited hairstyle is held in place by a diadem; the strands of hair are tied at the back of the head into a distinctive bun worn only by kings. The exquisite finish is in clear contrast to the signs of violence that have scarred the head. Eyes

Cast copper alloy head of a king, Nineveh, *c.* 2200 BC.

that were originally inlaid, perhaps with shell and a dark stone for the pupils, have been removed, a gaping hole at the left eye the result of multiple blows from a chisel. A similar tool was used to attack the upper bridge of the nose and the point of the nose has been flattened by several blows from a hammer. Both ears have been cut and broken off by strong chisel blows. This very deliberate destruction was designed to do more than simply mutilate an inanimate object. Mesopotamian images were believed to contain something of the living essence of the figures depicted and so here the action was an attack on the kings of Agade themselves, removing their sight, hearing and smell. It is possible that the sculpture had been set up in Nineveh, perhaps on the orders of Manishtushu, or it may simply have reached the city as part of plunder in the dying days of the empire.

Independent city states re-emerged across the region. We see this most clearly in northern Mesopotamia at Mari, which established itself as the centre of a flourishing kingdom. While the most widespread languages spoken were probably Semitic, there were also numbers of people speaking a very different language known as Hurrian, perhaps moving into north Syria from the highlands to the north and establishing their own small states. In the far south of Babylonia the rulers of the city of Ur claimed supremacy over the alluvium and extended their authority eastwards, controlling a crucial region between the Tigris and the Zagros Mountains. Known today as the Third Dynasty of Ur (or Ur III), the kingdom reached its greatest extent under King Shulgi (*c.* 2090–2050 BC). As under the Agade empire, it is unclear if Ashur was ruled directly from the south as a province or whether the local rulers recognized the kings of Ur. But there were certainly diplomatic connections further north; an inscription records the marriage of a princess of Nineveh to Shulgi's grandson Shu-Sin. In this way Nineveh enters history as an independent state. It was ruled by a man with the Hurrian name of Tish-atal, who is described in the Ur III records as 'the man of Nineveh'.[15] He undertook a visit to southern Babylonia in the third year of Shu-Sin, arriving with an entourage of more than one hundred men. This was followed by the marriage of Ti'amat-bashti, likely his daughter, to Shu-Sin. An earlier offering made at Ur to the Hurrian goddess Shaushka of Nineveh in Shulgi's 46th year is clearly also a reflection of these diplomatic relations.

The centralized control of the Ur III state started to weaken during the reign of Ibbi-Sin (*c.* 2028–2004 BC). This was the result of a number of factors that, according to correspondence between the king and his officials, included shortages of grain and disruption to the routes of communication and supplies by mobile groups of pastoralists. Around 2004 BC a coalition of forces from kingdoms in western Iran, including an army from the powerful kingdom of Elam, attacked Ur, occupied the city and captured Ibbi-Sin.

Relief of the god Assur, Ashur, *c.* 1500 BC.

THREE
Merchants and Kings

The collapse of Ur's kingdom was remembered in later literary accounts as a catastrophe comparable with the famous mythical Flood sent by the gods. These so-called Lamentations, composed several centuries after the events they claim to describe, may capture something of the crisis and disorder that brought invading armies into Babylonia even if the historical detail is imagined. What is certain, however, is that the end of the Ur III state removed the centralized systems of taxation and trade that had maintained it. New centres of power emerged in Babylonia but none that could match the wide-ranging authority of the earlier kingdom. Meanwhile, further north, Ashur was also impacted by these major political and economic upheavals but the changes that resulted ultimately came to benefit the city, enabling it to acquire great wealth.

Trade had, of course, long played a major role in the life of Ashur's community. This included long-distance commercial activity, especially the import of tin (for combining with copper to make bronze) together with the vibrant blue stone lapis lazuli from mining areas as far east as Afghanistan. In the decades after 2000 BC, new opportunities emerged for Ashur's merchants to build on their existing trading networks and they were quick to seize them. Inscriptions set up at this time by a succession of Ashur's kings boast of prosperity based on trade with Babylonia and indicate that merchants were being actively encouraged to come to the city to sell and buy.

Ashur's role as a great trading centre becomes very apparent from the contents of some 23,000 cuneiform texts that document in extraordinary detail an aspect – albeit a major part – of an international trade network run out of the city. The clay tablets were not discovered in Ashur but excavated at a colony that had been established by Assyrian merchants outside the walls of the city of Kanesh (modern Kültepe in eastern Turkey) many weeks' journey to the west.[1] This traders' district is named in the texts as Karum Kanesh, meaning 'Kanesh harbour', and it acted as the administrative centre of a colonial network of Assyrian merchants reaching across central Anatolia. Their focus was on the import of woollen textiles (manufactured in Ashur and Babylonia) and tin in exchange for local silver and gold.

The time period covered by the Kanesh administrative documents, which are household archives consisting largely of the correspondence between merchants and their families and business associates in Ashur, is approximately 1960 to 1840 BC. These, together with the evidence from excavations at both Kanesh and Ashur, allow us remarkable insights into the world of the Karum and its home city and the lives of some of their inhabitants. Let us start our exploration in Ashur itself during the reign of King Sargon I (*c.* 1920–1881 BC), when trade peaked and by which time the resulting wealth and investment in splendid new buildings in the city may have encouraged the ruler to adopt as his throne name that of the famous earlier king of Agade.

Despite its prosperity, Ashur was a small town of about 50 hectares (about the size of Vatican City) with perhaps 7,000 inhabitants – although a good number of these lived in the trading colonies. The city appears to have been governed in a very different way to the city states elsewhere in the region with their palaces from which rulers undertook seasonal military campaigns for plunder and tribute. While there was a hereditary monarchy in Ashur, there is no evidence for a specific royal building, nor for political and military interactions with the city's neighbouring states. Instead, the king seems to have functioned as the principal officer – rather like a chairman – of the City Assembly, the main administrative institution. He was called '*ensi* of Ashur', a title used for city governors under the Ur III kingdom.[2] Now, however, the writing of 'Ashur' in inscriptions starts to include a cuneiform sign that indicates it should be understood as the name of a god. In this way, deity and city become fused – to avoid confusion going forward, the spelling 'Assur' will be used in this book for the name of the god and 'Ashur' for his city. The ruler was viewed simply as the steward of Assur, who was the real king, described as 'the great one', and 'overseer', who would come to be represented as the very escarpment on which the city was built, dominated at its highest point by his temple. A relief of a later date from Ashur, for example, depicts the god Assur as a bearded man with his lower body formed by a scale pattern, a traditional Mesopotamian way of indicating mountains.[3] He holds in each hand a branch that ends in buds or perhaps pine tree cones, which goats nibble. Two smaller figures have vases from which flow mountain streams.

The City Assembly over which the king presided was a court of law to which traders could appeal. On these occasions the Assembly met in a sacred space behind the temple of Assur but other business was probably conducted in the City Hall, where the finances of the city were managed. Frustratingly, there is no indication in the texts of who was eligible for membership of these institutions but a very important official was the *limum*, the director of the City Hall, who changed each year.

Although much of the wealth of the city was generated by the merchant families of Ashur, foreigners also came to the city to trade but didn't stay. Elamites from southwest Iran exchanged tin for gold and Babylonians sold textiles (treaties ensured that they couldn't trade elsewhere). Others who found a market for their raw materials and finished goods were Amorites (living in towns and villages across the steppe to the northwest) and Subaraeans (Hurrian-speakers to the northeast of Ashur), but these people – by decision of the City Hall – were not permitted to be paid in gold.

The main currency of exchange was silver. The metal was used to buy barley (a necessary import given Ashur's limited agricultural land) and wool, the latter brought to the city by so-called Suhu nomads who grazed extensive flocks of sheep across the steppe. The sheep were herded on a seasonal basis to the pasture around Ashur, where their wool was plucked rather than shorn. Female members of the different merchant families bought the wool and wove it into textiles in their homes. The technical skill of the weavers was very important since they needed to be able to copy different techniques of weaving in response to demand. Finished textiles were then cleaned and entrusted to male members of their family, who either travelled regularly to the colonies themselves or made use of paid transporters who might be moving a range of goods.

There were Assyrian merchants operating at all levels with a few important and very wealthy dealers to whom the king and senior officials entrusted goods in order to earn profits. These merchants might in turn employ agents who acted as middlemen, ensuring there were porters and guides and that their wages were paid. Key to the operation were donkeys that were loaded with the bales of cloth as well as panniers containing tin and lapis lazuli for the long journey to the west. Many people were employed in raising and training the animals in paddocks outside the city, while others produced their harnesses and other equipment needed for supporting the caravans.

When all was in place, lines of donkeys would depart. They set off across the region known today as the Jezira 'island', the undulating steppe land between the Tigris and Euphrates. Turning north, the caravans would thread their way through the foothills of the Taurus Mountains onto the Anatolian plateau. The authorities in Ashur established treaties with local rulers who charged tolls and duties, ensured security and agreed compensation for any losses that occurred in their territory. Mirroring these regulations, a shadowy system of contraband also existed, either to avoid paying the taxes or in order to trade restricted products. In the mountainous paths, some merchants might take a detour away from authorized routes and checkpoints, but this, of course, left them exposed to attack from highway robbers and wild animals. Others might choose not to declare taxable goods or make a partial declaration by paying off local officials.

At its height, the system consisted of some thirty trading centres spread across central Anatolia and another ten along the caravan roads of north Mesopotamia. Some colonies were established near or in the mining areas for copper and this allowed the Assyrians to involve themselves in the local trade in the metal

Clay tablet (*left*) and its sealed envelope. The table records a legal dispute, from Karum Kanesh, *c.* 1950–1850 BC.

to make additional profit. Kanesh, however, was the hub of the system and the initial focus for many caravans. On arrival at the city, goods would be inspected by the palace officials, who would charge transport and import taxes as well as residency fees; the king of Kanesh was also given first pick of the goods. The donkeys might then be sold and the remaining goods prepared for sale locally or for export to other trading stations.

The city of Kanesh was around four times the size of Ashur with a population of about 30,000 people. Foreign merchants, some 3,000 in number with the majority from Ashur, occupied their own district in a lower town. This was the Karum, where many merchants lived for several years at a time. It had its own office that kept in touch with the other Assyrian trading posts via messengers, maintained contact with local rulers, and regulated and taxed activities of individual traders. The Karum also needed to maintain close connections with the government in Ashur, whose decisions it had to communicate and implement. Crucially, it acted as a law court and dealt with conflicts between its members or appeals to reverse decisions made by other colonies. The Karum Kanesh tablet shown here, for example, along with its clay envelope, records the court testimony in a dispute between two merchants, Suen-nada and Ennum-Assur. It starts with a statement by Suen-nada: 'While I and my maidservant stayed in Kanesh, you [Ennum-Assur] went off to Durhumit [another Assyrian colony], and although I owe you nothing you acted high-handedly and entered my guesthouse and took out 2 containers sealed by me as well as the objects.'[4] There then follows a list of the contents of the containers, which comprised 23 tablets each recording the details of business transactions, such as the amounts of silver owed by Suen-nada to other merchants, as well as cylinder seals of individuals who had deposited them with Suen-nada for safe keeping.

Ennum-Assur responds:

> When my agent Idi-Ishtar died three years ago, and in spite of the fact that you had no claim on either me or my agent Idi-Ishtar, without the permission of either the harbour or the merchants present here, you high-handedly entered the house of my agent Idi-Ishtar in the Durhumit harbour, he who owed some 5 talents of silver or more to me, and you robbed the strongroom of my agent – ever since then I have been chasing you and repeatedly sent witnesses for you, and they have bound you over. Three years have now passed, and the Kanesh harbour has learned of your robbery and your lies, and after they have had you yourself and your partners extradited to the Kanesh harbour, and I have stated formally under oath in the Kanesh harbour to you and your partners the facts about the robbery and the lies, and after our tablets were written a month ago and were entrusted to the bureau of the harbour, stating that I have not entered your house and have not taken anything belonging to you – after all this you go on asking me questions in court concerning my tablets!

Both men declare that they had given their testimony 'before Assur's dagger', which was understood as a living extension of the god, and Ennum-Assur then calls for the case to be moved to Ashur so that it can be tried in front of the City Assembly and king. The testimony having been recorded, presumably by a court scribe, the tablet was enclosed in the clay envelope that was sealed across the front, back and sides with the cylinders of two witnesses; the impressions show so-called presentation scenes in which a worshipper approaches a seated god who holds a cup. Frustratingly, the verdict of the court case remains unknown.

The Kanesh tablets offer much more than just legal disputes; letters and other documents reveal the lives of Assyrian families, including the wives of merchants. They usually stayed behind in Ashur, managing their households and raising their children, while their husbands were conducting business in Anatolia. Although marriage was monogamous, Assyrian merchants who settled in the colonies for several years might take a second wife for the length of their stay, but this probably would have only applied to merchants who were sufficiently wealthy to afford two households. Most wives were involved in the business operation, which might, as we have seen, involve the weaving of cloth for sale and for which they received payment and kept the money. One rather exasperated woman, for example, wrote to her critical and demanding husband,

> As to the textiles about which you wrote to me on the following terms: 'they are too small, they are not good'; was it not on your own request that I reduced the size? Now you write again, saying 'process half a mina of wool more in your textiles.' Well, I have done it.[5]

Indeed, women and men appear as equals: both were permitted to initiate divorce proceedings; they paid identical fines when laws were broken; both could lend money and buy and sell houses as well as slaves, the latter appearing in sale contracts, wills and divisions of inheritance and considered a sign of wealth in both Ashur and Kanesh.

From around 1860 BC the volume of written evidence from Kanesh starts to shrink. This appears to be partly a response to the changing commercial situation as other colonies came to replace Kanesh as significant trading hubs, especially those located closer to copper mines in the north and west (such as Durhumit, the place mentioned in the legal case). But there were clearly also major political challenges from rival states in the region; in around 1835 BC the city of Kanesh itself was destroyed and with it the Assyrian Karum.

Amorites and Hurrians

It was not only in Anatolia that politics intruded violently into the lives of the Assyrians. By the end of the nineteenth century BC the city of Ashur was swept up in the ambitions of rival kings, especially those of an Amorite ruler called Samsi-Addu (the Assyrian form of the name is Shamshi-Adad). His power base may have been the city of Ekallatum, about 30 kilometres (19 mi.) north of Ashur. Samsi-Addu had a powerful rival in the king of Eshnunna who controlled territory around the junction of the rivers Tigris and Diyala and it may have been tensions between the two small states that forced Samsi-Addu early in his reign to seek refuge in Babylon, where he probably had connections with the royal family. Around 1810 BC, however, he retook Ekallatum, and then three years later advanced along the Tigris and captured Ashur, removing King Erratum II.

This was the start of some fifteen years of conquest in which Samsi-Addu extended his authority over the Jezira, culminating in the defeat of Mari around 1792 BC. Appointing his eldest son Ishme-Dagan as viceroy of Ekallatum a few years later, he selected a city called Shehna (modern Tell Leilan in northeast Syria) as his capital and renamed it as Shubat-Enlil ('the residence of the god Enlil'). This was a strategic location as it allowed Samsi-Addu to control the important Jezira caravan routes and thus the wealth of Ashur.

At Ashur itself Samsi-Addu rebuilt the temple of Assur, which now was provided with two shrines, one for Assur and one for Enlil (supreme god of the Babylonian pantheon), which not only reflected Samsi-Addu's southern connections, but established a close relationship between the two deities.[6] In his inscriptions, written in Babylonian cuneiform rather than Assyrian, Samsi-Addu grandly calls himself 'king of the universe' and 'appointee of the god Enlil', but he also retained the traditional Assyrian title of '*ensi* of Assur'. Towards the end of his reign he extended his control over Nineveh, where he refurbished the temple of Ishtar: 'I erected the doorframes of that temple, the equal of which for perfection no king had ever built, for the goddess Ishtar of Nineveh'.[7]

After Ishme-Dagan had ascended the throne on the death of his father around 1775 BC, the western half of the kingdom slipped out of his control and was taken by Zimri-Lim of Mari. The loss of a large area of the Jezira must have been keenly felt by the merchants of Ashur as it would have demanded a reorganization of the trade routes and new treaties negotiated across the region. Things became even more complicated for them in about 1770 BC when the ruler of Eshnunna led an army north and defeated Ishme-Dagan's forces, reducing his control to the region of Ashur and Ekallatum. Good relations were, however, maintained with Hammurabi, the ruler of Babylon, who received military support from

Fragment of victory stele possibly showing Samsi-Addu I defeating his enemy, *c.* 1800 BC.

Ishme-Dagan, now in the final years of his reign. At this point or soon after, Hammurabi initiated a rapid conquest of Babylonia and Eshnunna and then, around 1760 BC, turned on his ally Mari. Ashur lay beyond the reaches of his extensive kingdom but both the city and Ishtar of Nineveh are mentioned in the prologue of Hammurabi's famous law code, suggesting that close political and religious ties between north and south were maintained.

Little is known about Ashur for the next two hundred years, although there was clearly much continuity: the functions of the City Hall were maintained and a line of rulers, albeit not from the family of Sami-Addu, used the title '*ensi* of Assur' with Assyrian cuneiform restored for official inscriptions. The same period witnessed changes in the political landscape across the wider region. Babylon's territory shrank following the death of Hammurabi and Ashur came under increasing pressure from the north, where a patchwork of states were increasingly linked through the overlordship of the kingdom of Mittani, known to the Assyrians as Hanigalbat. Centred on the rich agricultural lands of northeast Syria, the rulers of Mittani belonged to the Hurrian-speaking population, which reached from the Mediterranean coastal areas of Syria eastward to the foothills of the Zagros Mountains, a region over which they extended their control. In the west this brought their armies into conflict with those of Egypt, which was imposing its authority over the small kingdoms of the southern Levant and sending military and hunting expeditions into Syria. In the east, Mittanian power extended to Nuzi and Arrapha (Kirkuk). Ashur, however, managed to retain its independence: inscriptions of the Egyptian pharaoh Thutmose III (1479–1425 BC) refer to deliveries of 'tribute' from Ashur, including lapis lazuli, stone vessels and horses with equipment, but this would be better understood as a greeting gift sent between kings. Indeed, gold was received from Egypt in return. Such diplomatic overtures may, however, have been the reason for a military response by King Saushtatar of Mittani (around 1430 BC), who, according to a later account, looted Ashur, carrying off a gold and silver door.[8]

Assyria and the brotherhood of kings

A chance for Ashur to shake off the authority of the Mittanian king occurred when rivalry among his successors for the throne led to a division of the kingdom. The weakening of Mittani meant that the Assyrian ruler Assur-uballit (1356–1322 BC) was able to describe himself as 'king', the first use of the title in Assyria since Samsi-Addu. It is significant, however, that Assur-uballit is described as 'king of the land of Assur' – authority was now based on his rule over territory, albeit still on behalf of the god Assur: later generations would regard this as the true moment of the birth of Assyria. The security of the state was ensured by extending the land of Assur, and Assur-uballit now annexed to his realm the important grain-growing regions to the north and east of Ashur, which included Nineveh and Arbela.

An ideology of kingship based on territorial expansion was one shared by the rulers of Egypt, Mittani, Babylonia (unified under a line of so-called Kassite kings) and Hatti (central Anatolia and northwest Syria, conquered by Hittite kings), all of whom called each other 'brother' in their mutual correspondence. Assur-uballit reached out to join this 'Club of Brothers' in a rather unprepossessing letter sent to the Egyptian pharaoh (possibly Amenhotep IV, 1356–1336 BC):[9]

> Say to the King of Egypt: 'Thus Assur-uballit, the king of Assyria. For you, your household, for your country, for your chariots and your troops, may all go well. I send my messenger to visit you and to visit your country. Up to now, my predecessors have not written; today I write to you. I send you a beautiful chariot, 2 horses, and a date-stone of genuine lapis lazuli, as your greeting-gift. Do not delay the messenger whom I send to you for a visit. He should visit and then leave for here. He should see what you are like and what your country is like, and then leave for here.'[10]

These were tentative beginnings but a second letter, perhaps a few years later, reveals a much more confident king, one who is happy

Letter of Assur-uballit I to the king of Egypt, *c.* 1350 BC.

to compare himself favourably with other members of the club with expectations of being treated as an equal 'brother':

> To . . . Great King, king of Egypt, my brother: 'Thus Assur-uballit, king of Assyria, Great King, your brother. For you, your household and your country may all go well. When I saw your messengers, I was happy. Certainly your messengers shall reside with me as objects of great solicitude. I send as your greeting-gift a beautiful royal chariot outfitted for me, and 2 white horses also outfitted for me, 1 chariot not outfitted, and

1 seal of genuine lapis lazuli. Is such a present that of a Great King? Gold in your country is dirt, one simply gathers it up. Why are you so sparing of it? I am engaged in building a new palace. Send me as much gold as is needed for its adornment. When Assur-nadin-ahhe, my ancestor, wrote to Egypt, 20 talents of gold were sent to him. When the king of Hanigalbat wrote to your father in Egypt, he sent 20 talents of gold to him. Now I am the equal of the king of Hanigalbat, but you sent me . . . of gold, and it is not enough for the pay of my messengers on the journey to and back. If your purpose is graciously one of friendship, send me much gold. And this is your house. Write me so what you need may be fetched. We are countries far apart. Are our messengers to be always on the march with only such results. As to your messengers having been delayed in reaching you, Suteans [nomads] had been their pursuers and they were in mortal danger. I detained them until I could write and the pursuing Suteans be taken for me. Surely my messengers are not to be delayed in reaching me. Why should messengers be made to stay constantly out in the sun and so die in the sun? If staying out in the sun means profit for the king, then let him [a messenger] stay out and let him die right there in the sun, but for the king himself there must be a profit. Or otherwise, why should they die in the sun? As to the messengers we have exchanged . . . do they keep my messengers alive? They are made to die in the sun!'[11]

While claims of friendship and the exchange of gifts were part of the diplomatic niceties between royal courts, these masked the political manoeuvring behind the scenes. So, for example, in the rivalry for the throne of Mittani, Assyria supported one candidate – who returned to Ashur the booty of Saushtatar – while the Hittites favoured another man whose power base was at Arrapha. This was a centre that was coveted by Assyria but also by Babylonia; attempts to control the east Tigris region, agriculturally rich with a crucial north–south trade route running through it and branches heading east, would be a constant source of friction between the two kingdoms. One means of stabilizing relations was through treaties reinforced by royal marriage and Assur-uballit's daughter was therefore wed to the Babylonian king Burnaburiash II (1359–1333 BC). Their young son succeeded as king of Babylonia but was killed in a rebellion and so Assur-uballit intervened militarily to replace the usurper (in the eyes of the Assyrians) with Kurigalzu II (1332–1308 BC), another son of Burnaburiash. From now on Assyrian–Babylonian relations would pivot between friendship and aggression.

Although the role of high priest of Assur remained paramount, Assyrian royal inscriptions increasingly stress the king's role as a military leader; Assur's dagger on which the merchants of Kanesh had sworn their oaths had been symbolically transformed into a sword wielded by the monarch. The curved sword shown here belonged to Adad-nirari I (1307–1275 BC), as indicated by the cuneiform inscription on both sides of the blade and along its non-cutting edge: 'Palace of Adad-nirari, king of the universe, son of Arik-den-ili, king of Assyria, son of Enlil-nirari, king of Assyria.'[12] The text is accompanied by an engraving of an antelope reclining on a platform, the meaning of which is unknown. Such swords are

Sword of Adad-nirari I, without provenance, *c.* 1300 BC.

depicted in Assyrian art in the hands of gods and kings and this one may have been intended for ceremonial use as much as for fighting. Yet the king would have also required a sharpened version as he was expected to lead his troops into battle. The vast majority of his army consisted of infantry conscripted from the tax-paying population as part of their obligations of service to him. Military campaigns were generally undertaken during the summer months when farm workers were less essential for agricultural activities and could leave their fields to fight. A more professional component of the army was the chariotry, which was led by members of the leading families who had the resources to maintain equipment and horses and the time to exercise their skill in using the bow and arrows with which they fought.

Throughout the thirteenth century BC, Assyrian kings extended their control over Mittanian territory to the west, where they also pushed back against Hittite influence in the region. Shalmaneser I (1269–1241 BC) was able to claim the final overthrow of Mittani and declared wide-ranging authority: 'Assur, the lord, faithfully chose me to worship him, gave me the sceptre, weapon, and staff to rule the black-headed people, and granted me the true crown of lordship.'[13] A network of fortresses was established across upper Mesopotamia and this became an important element in enabling regular campaigns to gain booty and tribute. It was, however, the military successes of Tukulti-Ninurta I (1240–1205 BC) that considerably enhanced the image of Assyrian kingship. Assyrian power was extended west into Hittite territory and, most spectacularly, south into Babylonia following tensions over the disputed territories east of the Tigris. Here the conflict escalated and the Assyrian king reports,

> I approached Kashtiliashu, king of Karduniash [Babylonia], to do battle. I brought about the defeat of his army and felled his warriors. In the midst of that battle I captured Kashtiliashu, king of Kassites, and bound I brought him as a captive into the presence of the god Assur, my lord. Thus I became lord of Sumer and Akkad in its entirety.[14]

The plundering of the great city of Babylon was celebrated not only in royal inscriptions but in a lengthy poem that was copied in Assyria for centuries, underlining the scale of the achievement.

The result of Assyrian kings campaigning in all directions resulted in an expansion in resources, and particularly an increase in the labour force made available from populations in their thousands that were deported from newly conquered territories. This enabled Tukulti-Ninurta to undertake major building works. He constructed an enormous palace at Ashur (the so-called New Palace) on a great platform. Some of the gods also received new homes in the city; the old Ishtar Temple, which the king's inscriptions describe as being 720 years old, was replaced by a building to the north of its former site and the temple to Sin (the moon god) and Shamash (the sun god of justice) was completely rebuilt.

The monuments of Tukulti-Ninurta depict his close association with the gods. Among the earliest surviving royal images from Ashur, for example, is a cult pedestal from the Ishtar temple (though it had probably originally been set up in the Assur temple). Carved in relief on one side is a representation of two bearded figures in

Cult pedestal of Tukulti-Ninurta I, Ashur, *c.* 1230 BC.

profile facing towards an altar that has the same form as the one that bears the scene. The pedestal is in fact a support for a divine symbol and is inscribed on its stepped base with a text of Tukulti-Ninurta. The fringed robes and mace identify both men in the scene as the king, his right hand raised with pointed figure in a distinctive Assyrian gesture of prayer. We therefore see Tukulti-Ninurta approaching and kneeling before the altar at the same time. A symbol shown on top of the carved altar may represent a clay tablet, and the tapering rod dividing it a writing stylus. The accompanying inscription states that the unceasing prayers of the king, perhaps imagined as written on the tablet, were repeated daily by Nusku, the god of light, in the presence of the gods Assur and Enlil. The scene is a continuous narrative; that is, the action takes place within the same space rather than in separate episodes as in a modern comic strip. The relief is thus a representation of the actual act of worship by the king. Through this very sophisticated use of space, the artist emphasizes the unceasing nature of the king's worship as stated in the inscription – there is nothing visually to disrupt his movement.[15]

Along with his major building projects at Ashur, Tukulti-Ninurta took the exceptional step of founding a new royal city. Constructed just 3 kilometres (almost 2 mi.) upstream of Ashur the king named it after himself: Kar-Tukulti-Ninurta. This may have been an attempt to free himself from the constraints of Ashur with its established traditions and nobility or simply an act of hubris. By any measure it was a massive undertaking. Surrounded by a vast wall with at least four gates, the city stretched over some 250 hectares (620 ac). It included a temple that brought together all the great gods of Assyria in one place: Assur, Adad (the storm god), Shamash, Ninurta (the warrior god), Nusku, Nergal (the plague god), the Sebitti ('the Seven' beneficent gods) and Ishtar. An enormous 'South Palace' was decorated with wall paintings of palmettes, rosettes, animals, stylized trees and bird-headed human spirits. And in order to provide the population of the city with water, Tukulti-Ninurta ordered the construction of a canal. In his words,

> I cut straight as a string through rocky terrain, with stone chisels I cleared a way through high and difficult mountains, I cut a wide path for a stream to support life in the land and provide abundance, I transformed the plains of my city into irrigated fields. From the produce of the waters of that canal I arranged for regular offerings for Assur and the great gods my lords in perpetuity.[16]

Although the official inscriptions describe a powerful, confident monarch, the contemporary administrative documents portray a less happy situation in which the absence of agricultural workers as a result of their recruitment for military campaigns led to poor harvests, while warfare itself led to large numbers of refugees. There were also recurring problems caused by raiders as well as ongoing resistance to Assyria from Babylonia and Elam. These factors may have contributed to internal unrest against the ageing monarch, at least at his court, and after over 35 years on the throne, Tukulti-Ninurta was assassinated. His new city was abandoned and the royal court returned to Ashur, where two of his sons and another claimant succeeded him in rapid succession. While these intrigues did not lead to the major loss of Assyria's territories across northern Mesopotamia, by around 1190 BC the Babylonian ruler, Adad-shuma-usur, felt sufficiently strong to mount a challenge to Assyria's claim to the southern kingdom and he captured the Assyrian king in battle.

In the same period the economic engine that had sustained the Club of Brothers began to falter and kingdoms to the west of Assyria began to succumb to internal and external pressures. The Hittite empire, faced by the collapse of their Anatolian vassals as well as raids from hostile groups, rapidly disintegrated, although some of their governors in southeast Anatolia and northern Syria maintained their control over what were now independent kingdoms. As central and southern Syria fragmented into small, widely spaced, urban centres, much of the plains were claimed by local tribal groups who spoke the Semitic Aramaic language. While Aramaeans populated the cities and farming villages, a large number were pastoral nomads, moving their animals across grazing lands that in the past had been largely managed and policed by the various state authorities. From the middle of the twelfth century BC probable changes in the climate, perhaps for only a few years, led to a drying of the pastureland. Settled agriculturalists living on the margins of farmland began to adopt more flexible mobile lifestyles and joined with the pastoralist groups who began to seek new grazing lands, inevitably bringing them into conflict with sedentary groups and disrupting communications. They started to penetrate Assyrian territories and repeated military campaigns were launched from Ashur and Nineveh against them.

Around 1100 BC Tiglath-pileser I (1114–1076 BC) undertook a triumphal march to the shores of the Mediterranean. With no strong state in Syria to bar his passage he crossed the river Euphrates – the first Assyrian king to do so – and reached the mountains of Lebanon, where cedars were felled and the beams sent back to Assyria for the refurbishment of a temple. The coastal cities of Byblos, Sidon and Arwad presented him with gifts. Such campaigns had, however, only short-term value as the real focus of Tiglath-pileser was on confronting Aramaean raiders – he claims in his inscriptions to have crossed the Euphrates 28 times in pursuit of them – but they were nearly impossible to control. The king also had to face aggression from the north, where he launched a campaign into the so-called Nairi lands in the region of Lake Van that combined deterrence with the goal of acquiring a supply of horses for the Assyrian army.

Although Tiglath-pileser undertook extensive building projects at Ashur – the Old Palace was refurbished with its walls lined with slabs of basalt, limestone and alabaster, while a new gatehouse was decorated with basalt statues of sea and mountain animals – the city was increasingly occupying a marginal position as Assyria confronted pressures from the north and west. The result was that Nineveh grew in importance. Here the king had a palace constructed that was decorated with glazed bricks, some of which represented palms, perhaps symbolizing divine abundance. Of particular interest, however, is the wall decoration in a second palace at Nineveh, where, according to Tiglath-pileser's inscriptions, were 'portrayed therein the victory and might which the gods Assur and Ninurta, the gods who love my priesthood, had granted me'.[17] These images have not survived but presumably represented scenes of battle, perhaps as narrative, in either sculpture, or glazed bricks, or paint. It is very possible that Nineveh, given the city's strategic significance, had become the primary royal residence.

The pressure on Assyria's borders remained relentless and the kingdom was further threatened by Babylonian forces when they captured a settlement close to Ashur. Tiglath-pileser was eventually able to expel them, but only after nearly a decade, when he took his revenge by plundering Babylon. By this time, however, Babylonia was also facing Aramaean incursions and its military efforts were directed against the bands of marauders pushing south following the Euphrates. By the time of Tiglath-pileser's death Aramaean groups may even have reached the heartland of Assyria.

FOUR

The Assyrian Empire

By the start of the tenth century BC, the Aramaean populations of the Syrian and north Mesopotamian plains had established large tribal states, leading to greater stability across the region. Earlier campaigns against them had resulted in a regular Assyrian presence in the fertile lands around the Khabur river, and Ashur-dan II (934–912 BC) now began to turn the tide in his favour. Territory was retaken and his successor Adad-nirari II (911–891 BC) was able to march south alongside the Euphrates to receive tribute from the various tribes and states straddling the river. The Assyrian revival led to a reopening of diplomatic relations with Babylonia and, late in his reign, Adad-nirari exchanged daughters in marriage with the Babylonian king Nabu-shuma-ukin. The Assyrian movement against hostile peoples encircling the kingdom continued under Tukulti-Ninurta II (890–884 BC). He maintained a strong presence in eastern Syria and was able to march through the region without apparent opposition. The same was true to the south, where the Assyrian king made a triumphal advance to the very border of Babylonia and received gifts from the local populations. The stage was set for the emergence of Assyria as the dominant power in the Middle East.

From Ashur to Kalhu

> The palace of Assurnasirpal, vice regent of Assur, chosen of the gods Enlil and Ninurta . . . with my cunning which the god Ea, king of the apsu, extensively wise, gave to me, the city of Kalhu [Nimrud] I took in hand for renovation. I cleared away the old ruin hill and dug down to the water level . . . I filled in the terrace. I founded therein a palace . . . as my royal residence, for my lordly leisure, decorated it in splendid fashion.[1]

With these words, carved in cuneiform over the front and back of a large rectangular sandstone block, Assurnasirpal II (883–859 BC) describes the establishment in the years around 870 BC of his new royal centre. This finely shaped free-standing monument was set up in a special niche adjacent to a gateway leading to the royal throne room of the very palace it describes.[2]

Kalhu was an ancient town lying beside the river Tigris and conveniently located at the heart of the Assyrian triangle. The transformation of its high settlement mound to create an imposing citadel with a royal residence would have certainly provided the town with considerable status since it could be included among a number of other Assyrian cities with a royal palace, not least Nineveh, where Assurnasirpal had been residing. On this occasion, however, the enormous investment in resources – both materials and human labour – to construct a new royal home represented a momentous and even revolutionary decision by the king; his aim was to replace the capital Ashur with Kalhu.

The text on the stela makes it clear that such a significant change was only possible thanks to the divinely inspired intelligence given to Assurnasirpal by Ea, the god of wisdom who lived in the subterranean freshwater ocean (*apsu*) on which the Earth was believed to rest. Indeed, the king needed the authority and support of the gods to undertake the move and, as the inscription informs us, to receive their blessings he ordered the rebuilding of Kalhu's existing temples. These belonged to: Ea, Damkina (Ea's wife), Adad, Shala (Adad's wife), Gula (the healing goddess), Nabu (the scribal god),

The 'Banquet Stela' of Assurnasirpal II, Kalhu (Nimrud), *c.* 870 BC.

Belet-nathi (the mother goddess), the Sibitti, and Ishtar-kidmuri (an aspect of the great goddess of sex and war). Perhaps more significantly, however, was the construction of new temples for two of Assyria's most powerful deities: Enlil (closely associated with Assur) and Ninurta (the son of Enlil). Assurnasirpal himself is shown at the top of the stela holding a staff of office, perhaps that of a shepherd, while placed before his face are divine symbols: the crescent of Sin, the winged disc of Shamash and to the rear of his head the star of Ishtar, a horned crown of Assur/Enlil, the forked lightning of Adad and seven dots representing the Sibitti.

This all signalled a new, exciting beginning for Assyria but at the same time certainly didn't break traditional royal connections with the city of Ashur since the god Assur remained there as the ultimate source of royal power. It was also the place to which the monarch would regularly return to undertake rituals of state and where on his death he would be buried. The question that clearly needs answering, however, is why, several centuries after Tukulti-Ninurta I's ultimately failed attempt to relocate the capital, did Assurnasirpal make this move? It may have been undertaken for very similar reasons to those of his predecessor, both symbolic and practical. Fundamentally, the refurbished city of Kalhu expressed the king's power and authority. Surrounded by a city wall enclosing an area of some 360 hectares (890 ac) with a walled citadel containing a massive mud-brick palace and temple buildings, it was intended to impress. It also underscored his military and diplomatic successes since it was these that provided him with the resources to make it possible.

When Assurnasirpal succeeded to the throne of Assyria in 883 BC, the kingdom was already established as the major power in northern Mesopotamia. He first moved to bring the mountainous territory to the north and northeast under his control, leading his forces along the valley of the Greater Zab and Tigris rivers to secure supplies of metals and horses. Military action also took place to the east, with the army pushing to the headwaters of the Diyala river, where a fortress called Dur Ashur was established as a strategic base in the Zagros Mountains. In the other direction, Assurnasirpal regularly led his army westwards to gather tribute and booty along the Khabur river, with campaigns launched further into Syria and that included, as he records in inscriptions set up in his palace, a crossing of the river Euphrates:

> I crossed the Euphrates, which was in flood, in rafts made of inflated goatskins and approached the land of Carchemish. I received tribute . . . 20 talents of silver, a gold ring, a gold bracelet, gold daggers, 100 talents of bronze, 250 talents of iron, bronze tubs, bronze pails, bronze bath-tubs, a bronze oven . . . beds, thrones, and dishes of boxwood decorated with ivory,

> 200 adolescent girls, linen garments with multi-coloured trim, purple wool . . . elephants' tusks, a chariot of polished gold, a gold couch with trimming . . . I took with me the chariots, cavalry, and infantry of the city of Carchemish. All the kings of the lands came down and submitted to me.[3]

The number of fortresses was expanded across the region for the storage and distribution of plunder and tribute, while huge numbers of people from eastern Syria and other regions were relocated to Assyria as agricultural workers and troops. Assurnasirpal's new city was thus the creation of forced labourers who were joined by Assyrians drafted in to complete corvée work they were obliged to undertake for their ruler.

On a practical level, however, relocating the capital was a means for Assurnasirpal to distance himself from the royal courts at Ashur and Nineveh with their established noble families and officials. The new city allowed the king to install his own choice of loyal servants and just as significantly it enabled him to fashion a new vision of kingship, one that was made very apparent through the magnificent decoration of his new palace. The result was that Kalhu would remain Assyria's primary royal residence for a century and a half, during which time the kingdom was transformed into a great empire.

Assurnasirpal may have established his court at Kalhu as early as 879 BC but it was probably many years before the massive building programme was completed.[4] The most magnificent structure was his new residence and centre of government, known today as the Northwest Palace from its location on the citadel mound. Overlooking the Tigris, it was an enormous mud-brick building more than 200 metres (656 ft) long and 118 metres (387 ft) wide, with state apartments, offices and private apartments organized around separate courtyards.[5] A stairway from the river may have provided access for people and goods arriving by boat. Approaching the palace from across the citadel a visitor – let us imagine an official with the necessary permissions – would have been faced by an outer wall and then passed through gateways and a series of courtyards before entering the great inner court. The palace walls are

Detail of a glazed brick from Kalhu showing the Assyrian king and courtiers, *c.* 870 BC.

likely to have been plastered gleaming white, with the crenellations and gateways embellished with glazed bricks with colourful floral or geometric designs, depictions of real and imaginary animals and images of the king. The glazed brick shown here originally formed part of a longer narrative scene in the Northwest Palace and shows Assurnasirpal standing beneath a fringed parasol and lifting a ritual bowl to celebrate his success in battle or the hunt (as indicated by the bow he holds in his left hand). The king, wearing the traditional truncated crown and fringed robes adorned with rosettes, is accompanied by officials and a soldier in a distinctive pointed helmet.

We know little about palace etiquette and how access to the king was managed.[6] The Northwest Palace is likely to have been a busy place with officials conducting business and organizing audiences with the monarch and other members of the royal family while servants catered for their needs. Our official may therefore have had to wait in the courtyard while ceremonies took place, tribute and reports were delivered and orders were given and recorded. This vast open space, which could have accommodated many hundreds of people, was dominated along its south side by the facade

Human-headed winged lion (*lamassu*), Northwest Palace, Kalhu, *c.* 870 BC.

of the throne room. This was punctuated by three great arched gateways, each of which was guarded by enormous stone sculptures of mythological creatures carved nearly in the round. These so-called *lamassus* (or *aladlammu*) were intended to provide powerful magical protection against dangerous, supernatural forces attempting to enter the palace. They take the form of human-headed winged bulls or lions depending on their placement at the gateways. Their heavily bearded human faces and long curling hair covering the shoulders express masculinity and strength and their headdresses with multiple pairs of bulls' horns indicate divinity. The largest figures consisted of winged bulls placed at right angles to the gates so that from the courtyard their bodies and faces were in profile. This orientation showed the creature's four striding legs but when somebody passed into or out of the gate the *lamassus* would have seemingly looked down at them, standing firm and unmoving with two front legs; it appears likely that these sculptures were intended to be viewed from either the front or the side rather than imagined as having five legs.

As we will explore in more detail, lions were closely associated with Assyrian kingship and the gateways of the throne room were supported by pairs of lion *lamassus*. They have a rope tied around their bodies just like those worn by mythological heroes who appear, for example, on cylinder seals and are also associated with the king. The *lamassus* guarding the gate on the left of the facade were carved with human arms, their hands clasped before them in a manner familiar from Assyrian representations of human attendants. The doorway gave access to the end of the throne room where there was a raised throne dais; this would have been partially visible from certain spots in the courtyard that may have been reserved for individuals sufficiently privileged to see the monarch seated in profile and facing to the right. The central facade gateway gave access to the throne room at a point where a stone slab was set into the floor and on which a temporary throne could be placed that faced into the courtyard; it was probably set up for specific occasions. Finally, the third gateway, on the right of the facade, had a pair of lion *lamassus* with human arms cradling a small deer. The walls adjacent to these sculptures were lined with a series of large stone panels carved in low relief showing a procession of foreign tributaries walking towards the king. The images suggest that this gate may have been the principal entrance through which people trooped for an audience with Assurnasirpal.

Entering the throne room is likely to have been an awe-inspiring experience that was designed to astonish and amaze. First, the double leaves of the gateway door were swung open. These were an astonishing 7 metres (23 ft) high and fashioned from sweet-smelling cedar, cypress or juniper wood and decorated with bronze bands.[7] Passing through the gate our official would have turned left to look down the length of the throne room towards the enthroned king in the distance. They would have been confronted by a vast space, measuring some 45.5 metres (150 ft) long, 10.5 metres (34 ft) wide and at least 10 metres (33 ft) high.[8]

The long southern wall of the throne room, illuminated to some extent by the light from the open doors, was lined with rectangular slabs of gypsum, some 2.5 metres high by 2 metres wide (8 by 6½ ft). These were carved in relief with images of the king overcoming the forces of chaos in the form of rebellious people and dangerous animals. They present a carefully designed, visually complex world, rich in details but always focusing on the image of the king. All the figures are carved in shallow relief and shown in profile against an undecorated background. And they were very colourful with details originally picked out with black, blue, red, white and green/yellow paint in parallel with paintings and glazed bricks that covered the plastered wall above the reliefs.[9] On his stela describing the creation of Kalhu, Assurnasirpal references these remarkable monuments that represent the earliest extensive use of such decoration in Assyria. 'I carved in a lapis lazuli-like stone on their walls my heroic praises, in that I had gone right across highlands, lands, and seas, and the conquest of all lands.'[10]

On entering the throne room through the right-hand door, our official would have first encountered carved scenes of a city under siege by the Assyrian army. The relief panels had two bands of carved images, each just over 1 metre high, separated by a somewhat narrower band carrying a cuneiform inscription. This text is known today as the Standard Inscription because it is repeated on nearly every wall slab in the Northwest Palace. It names Assurnasirpal, including his titles and those of his royal ancestors, his role as the priest and ruler chosen by the gods, his successful military campaigns, and the building work in Kalhu.

Walking towards the throne, the official passed more images of the king in action: his triumphal return from battle and a parade of captives, beyond which were depictions of him leading a chariot attack and crossing a river, probably the Euphrates. At this point our visitor would have come level with the central door and the throne base set into the floor. The narrative images on the walls are interrupted here by a single enormous wall panel carved with an iconic image of Assyrian kingship. At its centre, acting as an axis for a balanced composition, is a so-called sacred tree, a protective symbol of divinely bestowed abundance comprising flowing streams and palmettes, closely associated with the goddess Ishtar. The tree is flanked by images of a standing king in profile facing it and gesturing towards a god in a winged disc floating above. At the rear of each of the royal figures is a winged spirit blessing him using purifying equipment, the detail of which we will return to below.

Beyond this impressive image the panels divided into registers resume with separate scenes of the king leading an attack on a walled city, the hunting of lions and bulls, and the aftermath of

Assurnasirpal II flanking a 'sacred tree' and praying to the god Assur/Shamash, throne room of the Northwest Palace, Kalhu, *c.* 870 BC.

these moments, with the presentation of booty and celebratory rituals conducted over dead animals. These reliefs were the closest images to the king himself when enthroned on the high dais. On the short wall behind him was an almost identical version of the massive relief panel positioned opposite the central gate.

The theatre of kingship that was played out in the magnificent throne room was perhaps supported by special effects. The opening of the great doorways may have been choreographed in order to illuminate parts of the throne room at different times, playing with light and shadow across the reliefs. This dramatic effect would have been complemented by the flickering light from torches, while in winter there would be the added glow from a brazier on wheels that was rolled along stone slabs set into the floor between the central and eastern throne daises to keep the king warm. Incense may have filled the air as well as perhaps music from stringed lyres and cymbals, resonating in the cavernous space alongside the voices of the king and attendants.

Additional decorative elements added to the splendour of the interiors of this and other palace rooms. Plaques and knobs of glazed terracotta were inserted as decorations into the walls a little above head height. The varied painted patterns on the plaques include palmettes, pomegranates, targets, guilloches, chevrons and borders of black and white squares, all probably having protective symbolism. Many of the designs as well as some of the imagery on the wall reliefs were also found on elaborate pieces of wooden furniture, not least the royal throne. These were covered in sheets of bronze and ivory and decorated with animal heads, while palm capitals in metal, ivory or stone were placed at the top of the tapering feet and below the cross-bar.

Leading from the throne room, and passing between more lion *lamassus*, a gateway led to another large room giving access to a courtyard flanked by chambers also lined with wall reliefs. The eastern side of the palace was apparently devoted to ritual use. In the chamber nearest to the throne room were over-life-size images of beardless courtiers holding ladles and what look like flywhisks but are actually aspirgilla – brush-like bundles that are dipped in holy water and shaken – used to purify the king and his weapons.

A senior courtier purifies Assurnasirpal II, Kalhu, *c.* 870 BC.

In the next room along, the king is shown flanked by winged spirits, so-called *apkallu*, who also purify the king but use a pine cone (possibly a symbol of the god Assur) as a sprinkler for liquid from a bucket. The sequence of rooms ends with a narrow corridor lined with reliefs of sacred trees and bird-headed *apkallu*. Here, at the furthest end of this chamber, the floor was waterproofed with bitumen so that liquids could be poured as libations. According to myth, the *apkallu* were associated with sages who, at the beginning of time, shared with humans the rules by which they should be organized, including the notion of kingship. The series of rooms may have therefore served to magically connect the living king with that moment when order was established, ensuring that he was in a purified state to appear in majesty in the throne room.[11]

In contrast, the west wing of the palace was devoted to banquets that celebrated the king's success in battle and the hunt. But this too was deeply rooted in ritual since the king undertook these acts on behalf and with the support of the gods. One such feast is captured on an incised ivory plaque that once decorated a throne in the Northwest Palace. The king is seated on a high-backed chair attended by a servant and two armed officials; before him are pairs of diners facing each other across low tables. On the far left, an official uses a fan to cool the contents, perhaps water or wine, of three vessels in a stand. Such celebrations could be on a truly lavish scale, such as when Assurnasirpal marked the official

Bird- and human-headed protective spirits (*apkallu*) blessing 'sacred trees', Kalhu, *c.* 870 BC.

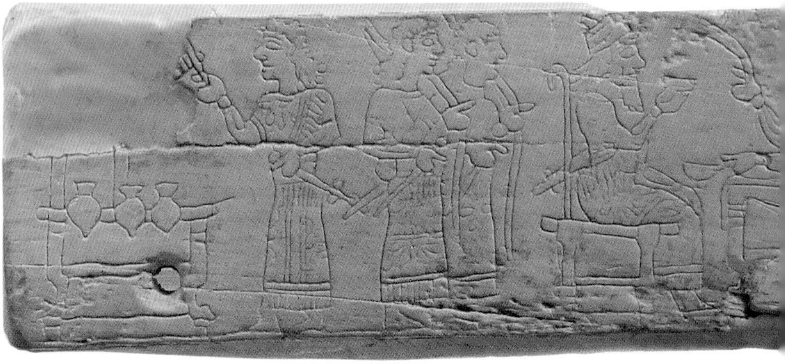

inauguration of his palace with tens of thousands of guests being provided with food and drink:

> When Assurnasirpal, king of Assyria, consecrated the joyful palace, the palace full of wisdom, in Kalhu and invited inside Assur, the great lord, and the gods of the entire land;
>
> 14,000 sheep, 100 lambs, 1,500 ducks, 1,000 deer, 500 geese, 10,000 pigeons, 10,000 turtle doves, 10,000 fish, 10,000 jerboa, 10,000 eggs, 10,000 loaves, 10,000 jugs of beer, 10,000 skins of wine, 10,000 containers of grain and numerous other foods, aromatics and beverages.
>
> When I consecrated the palace of Kalḫu, 47,074 men and women who were invited from every part of my land, 5,000 dignitaries and envoys of the people of the lands Suhu, Hindanu, Patinu, Hatti, Tyre, Sidon, Gurgumu, Malidu, Hubushku, Gilzanu, Kummu, and Musasiru, 16,000 people of Kalhu, and 1,500 employees of my palace, all of them – altogether 69,574 including those summoned from all lands and the people of Kalhu – fourteen days I gave them food, I gave them drink, I had them bathed, I had them anointed. Thus did I honour them and send them back to their lands in peace and joy.[12]

It is possible that many of the king's guests stood in wonder before the huge carvings and reflected not only on the Assyrian king's obvious power and wealth but on his benevolence, just like that of the gods.

Incised ivory plaque showing a royal banquet, Kalhu, *c.* 870 BC.

The Assyrian king

> The god Assur, the father of the gods, gave me [Esarhaddon] the power to let cities fall into ruins and to repopulate them, and to enlarge Assyrian territory; the god Sin, lord of the crown, decreed heroic strength and robust force as my fate; the god Shamash, the light of the gods, elevated my important name to the highest rank; the god Marduk, king of the gods, made the fear of my kingship sweep over the mountain regions like a dense fog; the god Nergal, mightiest of the gods, gave me fierceness, splendour, and terror as a gift; and the goddess Ishtar, the lady of battle and war, gave me a mighty bow and a fierce arrow as a present.[13]

At the heart of the emerging Assyrian Empire was the king. He was the supreme source of justice, shepherd and defender of his people, and, as high priest, he was intermediary between them and the gods. Assyrian rulers could claim a line of descent that stretched back over a thousand years, a fact recorded officially in the scholarly compiling of king lists. Indeed, the very office of kingship itself was understood to be part of the fabric of the cosmos, a concept lowered from heaven to earth soon after the world had been created. Given that the monarch's authority ultimately derived from the gods he was expected to act heroically in their name, ensuring that the universe was kept in order through force of arms in both battle and the hunt as well as by dispensing justice. Understandably, he played a central role in state rituals that often incorporated sophisticated allusions to mythological tales involving the gods, their public performances helping to underline the notion that the king ruled with divine support. Here the city of Ashur remained fundamentally important as the cultural and religious centre of Assyria. As home to the supreme god Assur, who lived in Esharra, 'Temple of the Universe', alongside temples for other gods and goddesses, there were regular cycles of festivals, many of which demanded the presence of the king.

Two of the greatest ritual events that took place at Ashur were the burial of a king and the coronation of his successor. The royal tombs were in vaults beneath the southeast wing of the so-called Old Palace, a building that not only evoked great antiquity but was the physical link between the temple of Assur and the city. Following the death of a monarch there would be a period of mourning before his burial with rich gifts. The dead were believed to enter an underworld where their spirit would find contentment if they were regularly supplied with offerings of food and drink by the living, the so-called *kispu* ritual, a duty that usually fell to their surviving family. This was no different for kings, except it was thought that they would sit for eternity in the presence of other past rulers (with presumably an expectation of the finest offerings).

Kingship passed from father to son – although we will discover that this was not always the case – and the transfer of authority took place with the blessing of Assur in his temple. It was here that the future king received the royal insignia, which were considered to be on loan from the gods. Some details of this momentous event are recorded in cuneiform texts.[14] The ceremony began with Assyria's nobles and the royal eunuchs performing some kind of ritual, after which the king processed from the palace to the Assur temple, described as the 'House of God': 'The carriers place the throne of the king upon their necks and set off for the House of God. They enter the House of God. The priest of Assur slaps the king's face in their presence and says thus: "Assur is king! Assur is king!"'[15]

The slapping was intended to stress the king's inferior status to Assur, who was the real ruler. The king now presented animal sacrifices to Assur as well as offerings of stones to a number of other deities (recalling perhaps a myth describing how the god Ninurta pronounced judgement on minerals, assigning them good or bad properties). A climax of the ceremony was reached as a priest placed the royal crown on the king's head and the nobles and royal eunuchs together recited the following words:

> May Assur and Mullissu [Assur's wife], the owners of your crown, cover you with your crown for a hundred years! May your foot be good in the temple and your hands be good at the chest of Assur, your God! May your priesthood and that of your sons be pleasing to Assur. Expand your country with your just sceptre! Expand your country with your just sceptre! May Assur give you command, understanding, obedience, justice and peace.[16]

The nobles then prostrated themselves before the king, kissing his feet. The new ruler left the temple and was carried back to the palace for the performance of another ritual before he was taken onto the palace terrace and seated on the royal throne. The nobles again prostrated themselves before him, kissing his feet and presenting gifts. This brought proceedings to a crucial moment when the king confirmed in post his most senior officials. The grand vizier and other courtiers set aside their symbols of office and stood apart, and the king addressed them with the words, 'Each and everybody keep his office!' This no doubt reflects the traditional script but perhaps in reality there was a moment of nervousness among the old guard as it offered the king an opportunity to replace them.

Crown prince, the future of Assyria

> You [Esarhaddon] have girded a son of yours with headband and entrusted to him the kingship of Assyria.[17]

When Assurnasirpal II came to the throne in 883 BC he stepped to the front of what was imagined to be an unbroken line of royal ancestors that reached back in time over a thousand years. The names of these earlier rulers were remembered through written lists and monuments. At Ashur, for example, stone stelae, averaging about 2 metres high and arranged in two groups, were each inscribed with either the name of an Assyrian king or that of a high official or, very rarely, a queen – over 140 survive dating from the fourteenth to the seventh centuries BC. These people had been honoured by having a calendar year named after them (whereas we use a sequence of numbers to refer to the years, the Assyrians used the names of the king and officers, known as *limmu*, in a fixed rotation) and their stone monuments both memorialized them and created a physical timeline. A much more straightforward record of earlier Assyrian rulers is, however, preserved in cuneiform documents known as king lists. These name over a hundred individuals with the lengths of their reigns.[18] The sense of dynastic continuity provided by these texts represented an important aspect of Assyrian kingship, one that certainly linked rulers with a distant past but, perhaps more importantly, gave them confidence in an assured future.

As with all monarchs who stress legitimacy through succession from father to son, the most important individual who ensured the continuity of Assyrian kingship was the crown prince. It should not come as a great surprise, therefore, that a recurring scene in the royal art of Assyria is an image of the king standing with a man who can be identified as his heir. The prince is recognizable by his beard and distinctive headband with two tasselled bands hanging down from the back.[19] This diadem marked him out as the king's son – but not necessarily the oldest – who had been selected by his father to succeed him; the headdress was presented as part of an investiture when the crown prince entered the so-called

House of Succession, a separate royal household with its own staff. From that point the crown prince would undertake specific duties – his was the second-highest position after the king's, outranking the commander-in-chief, the chief cupbearer and the treasurer – reporting directly to the monarch either from within Assyria itself or from the provinces, thereby acquiring a good knowledge of the regions he would eventually govern.

In the detail of a relief from the throne room of the Northwest Palace at Kalhu shown here, the crown prince stands on the right wearing fringed robes similar to those of Assurnasirpal, who faces him. The garments indicate that a ritual is taking place, one that marks the restoration of cosmic order by the king through the force of his arms, represented by the bow and arrows he holds. To achieve this result, he is supported by the gods, and indeed, hovering

Assurnasirpal and the god Assur/Shamash face the crown prince, Kalhu, *c.* 870 BC.

between father and son is a deity in a winged disc, perhaps a combination of the winged disc of Shamash, the sun god of justice, and Assur, who holds out the divine ring of kingship as if to the crown prince. This transfer of power occurred on Assurnasirpal's death in 859 BC and his heir was crowned king and took the throne name of Shalmaneser (the third Assyrian king with that name).

The royal inscriptions understandably tend to ignore or obscure any tensions at the royal court that might have accompanied the change of kings, and so what appears to us as a completely smooth transition may not have mirrored reality. The death of a monarch and the appointment of another were always moments of danger since they offered opportunities for rival claimants to try and seize power or for conquered populations to make a bid for independence.

Let's explore a few such moments of transition, starting in the mid-eighth century BC when Assyria's military fortunes had taken a turn for the worse. There had been a prolonged period of civil war as well as plague and major military defeats inflicted by the neighbouring kingdom of Urartu (dominating eastern Turkey and Armenia). The resulting loss of royal prestige led in 746 BC to a major rebellion at Kalhu and the overthrow of Assur-nirari V. The new king, Tiglath-pileser III (744–727 BC), was probably a member of the royal family but certainly not the crown prince. It is significant that he chose a throne name that evoked the powerful king of the late twelfth to early eleventh century BC. In its original Assyrian, however, the name Tukulti-apil-Esharra means 'my trust belongs to the son of the Esharra temple'. This refers to the warrior god Ninurta, the son and heir of Assur. In this way the new ruler linked himself to the heavenly crown prince and in doing so neatly sidestepped referencing his father in the inscriptions, the traditional way Assyrian kings stressed their legitimacy.

Tiglath-pileser transformed Assyria's fortunes by confronting Urartu and expanding Assyrian control in all directions beyond its traditional boundaries. In the wall reliefs from the palace he constructed at Kalhu, Tiglath-pileser presents himself at the centre of activity, but rather than depicting symbolic statements of conquest and triumph as in earlier sculptures, the focus is now on the defeat of real enemies, identified by cuneiform captions, within defined landscapes. Scenes of battles and cities under siege as well as the aftermath with captives and animals under escort and the presentation of tribute and booty to the king are favourite subjects. A very prominent role is given to the crown prince in such scenes, perhaps intended to make the point that, despite his own rather dubious route to the throne, Tiglath-pileser placed great store on convention.[20] At some point, he promoted a son called Ululayu to the position of heir apparent, and when the king died of natural causes in 727 BC the crown prince became Shalmaneser V (726–722 BC) without any challenge.

Yet history appeared to repeat itself. Five years into his reign, Shalmaneser was overthrown by his brother in what may have been another palace coup. The usurper took the celebrated name of Sargon (721–705 BC), becoming the second Assyrian monarch to connect themselves in this way with the famous third-millennium BC king of Agade. However, given that the name means 'the king is legitimate' its adoption may also be understood as special pleading by the new ruler. Convention had again been broken and for several years Sargon faced considerable opposition from inside Assyria as well as from the provinces. He set out, therefore, to present his rule as a new beginning for Assyria. Sargon acquired land some 45 kilometres (30 mi.) to the northeast of the capital and, mirroring Assurnasirpal's establishment of Kalhu 170 years earlier, he ordered the construction of a vast new palace and temple complex that was named Dur-Sharrukin – Fortress of Sargon (modern Khorsabad).[21] In this magnificent setting he relied heavily on trusted members of his immediate family, elevating his brother to the important role of grand vizier and his son Sennacherib to the position of crown prince.

The figure of a crown prince appears repeatedly on the palace wall reliefs at Dur-Sharrukin, where he is shown introducing long lines of officials and tribute bearers into the presence of the king. As at Kalhu under Tiglath-pileser III, these images were probably intended to demonstrate the continuity of the royal family after such a turbulent period, but in addition it highlighted the great wealth being brought to Sargon from across his vast realm. We know

much more about the role of the crown prince at this time since a number of letters sent from Sennacherib to his father survive. They would have been written on behalf of the crown prince by his senior scribes and delivered to Sargon, who was often away from the capital on campaign or visiting conquered territories. They include questions for the king to answer as well as reports on local and regional matters; all begin with a specific greeting used only by the crown prince. For example, this letter was sent to Sargon while he was in Babylon:

> To the king my lord: your servant Sennacherib. Good health to the king, my lord! Assyria is well, the temples are well, all the king's forts are well. The king, my lord, can be glad indeed.
>
> The emissaries of Commagene [in southeast Turkey] have come, bringing tribute and with it seven teams of mules. The tribute and the mules are entrusted to the Commagenean embassy, and the emissaries too are there, eating their bread.
>
> Should they [the tribute and the mules] be picked up and brought to Babylon, or can they be received here? Let them immediately write me what the king my lord commands.[22]

Here is part of another letter from Sennacherib that includes an intelligence report from an agent based near the border with Urartu:

> Assur-resuwa has written to me thus: 'The previous report which I sent about the Urartians was that they suffered a terrible defeat. Now his country is quiet again and each of his nobles has gone to his province. Kaqqadanu, his commander-in-chief, has been taken prisoner; the Urartian king is in the province of Wazaun.'[23]

Sargon's ambition that Assyrian kingship would be maintained into the future from Dur-Sharrukin ended with his death in battle in 705 BC. Such an inauspicious event – made especially so by the

Opposite: Sargon II facing his crown prince Sennacherib, Dur-Sharrukin, *c.* 710 BC.

fact that the king's body was not recovered and therefore couldn't be given an appropriate burial – had the potential to unleash a period of turmoil, but Sennacherib had consolidated his position as crown prince sufficiently so that there was no challenge to his accession. He acted quickly, though, to disassociate himself from his father's capital and shifted the royal court to the very ancient and venerable settlement of Nineveh. Over ten years the city was transformed into a glorious metropolis worthy of a ruler able to draw on resources from across much of the Middle East. The stone relief panels that lined the walls in Sennacherib's great Southwest Palace are covered with carved scenes of battle and victory while the generic figure of the crown prince appears in his usual role of presenting people to the king. By the time the palace was completed around 693 BC Sennacherib may have already appointed his son Urdu-mullissu to that role.

The immediate future of Assyrian kingship may have seemed settled but behind the scenes there were intrigues at court, perhaps even rival factions, jostling for privilege and influence – in the words of a later text, the royal princes 'butted heads for power'.[24] By the later 680s BC, this plotting may have even reached the ears of the king. A letter sent from Babylonia which may date to this period appears to suggest that Urdu-mullissu was contemplating patricide. A temple worker, having overheard talk of a planned rebellion against Sennacherib, approached two Assyrian officials, who asked him, 'What is your appeal to the King about?' He replied, 'It is about prince Urdu-mullissu.' In an account straight from a cloak-and-dagger thriller, the man was blindfolded and brought into the presence of a man he assumed would be the king. However, 'They covered his face with a cloak and made him stand before Urdu-mullissu, saying, "Behold, your appeal is granted; say it with your own voice!" He said: "Your son, Urdu-mullissu, is going to murder you!"' Unsurprisingly, it did not end well for the informant: 'They uncovered his face, and after Urdu-mullissu had interrogated him, they killed him and his brothers.'[25] The court may have become a dangerous place as conspiracy, accusation and misdirection swirled, and as a result Sennacherib's younger son Esarhaddon later claimed to have removed himself to a province somewhere in the west.

Things came to a head in 681 BC when, as recorded tersely in the so-called Babylonian Chronicle, 'on the twentieth day of the month of Tebet [December–January] Sennacherib, king of Assyria, was killed by his son in a rebellion'.[26]

Civil war engulfed Assyria for over forty days as rival forces gathered around Esarhaddon and Urdu-mullissu and their armies clashed in eastern Syria. By 680 BC Esarhaddon (680–669 BC) had emerged with sufficient support from within Assyria so that he was able to enter Nineveh and claim the throne. Although the regicide is not named by the Chronicle, it might have been Urdu-mullissu, especially if his position as crown prince was under threat. This is certainly the narrative as understood by the later compilers of the Hebrew Bible, who record, 'One day, while he [Sennacherib] was worshiping in the temple of his god Nisrok, his sons Adrammelek [Urdu-mullissu] and Sharezer killed him with the sword, and they escaped to the land of Ararat [Urartu]. And Esarhaddon his son succeeded him as king' (2 Kings 19:37).

The murder may have equally been engineered by Esarhaddon, who, having secured the throne, disseminated through official and unofficial channels an account that accused his brothers. There followed a mass execution of Esarhaddon's opponents. He spent the next eight years campaigning to maintain the borders of his empire: defeating resistance in southern Turkey, pushing into Iran and eastern Arabia and conquering the city of Sidon. After a failed first attempt, his greatest triumph, however, was the invasion of Egypt in 671 BC, driving the Pharaoh Taharqa out of the capital, Memphis. This success came a year after Esarhaddon had put into effect a plan for his succession that was aimed at finding a solution to the recurring problem of rivalry for the throne from within the royal family, as well as managing the often tricky relationship between Assyria and Babylonia. His novel solution was to divide Mesopotamia between two of his sons: Assurbanipal would become king of Assyria and Shamash-shumu-ukin king of Babylon.

To emphasize the significance of this arrangement, the appointment of Assurbanipal as crown prince of Assyria was stage-managed in a most elaborate manner. It involved a public ceremony on an almost unimaginable scale at which representatives of the different peoples of the empire swore an oath of allegiance to the young man. On 12 Ayr (March–April) 672 BC, proceedings commenced at Kalhu. Given the number of people involved, the event was repeated over several days. The oath was a legal treaty binding both Assyrians and their vassals to acknowledge and support Assurbanipal as the future Assyrian king. It was presumably recited out loud but the contents were also written down on large cuneiform tablets so that each contingent attending the ceremony could take one home with them as a record of the agreement. Around ten copies of this so-called succession treaty have survived, finely written in cuneiform. The first sections of the oath make its intentions very clear:

> This is the treaty which Esarhaddon, king of Assyria, has concluded with you, in the presence of the great gods of heaven and earth, on behalf of Assurbanipal, the great crown prince designate, son of Esarhaddon, king of Assyria, your lord, whom he has named and appointed as crown prince. When Esarhaddon, king of Assyria, passes away, you will seat Assurbanipal, the great crown prince designate, upon the royal throne, and he will exercise the kingship and lordship of Assyria over you. You shall protect him in country and in town, fall and die for him. You shall speak with him in the truth of your heart, give him sound advice loyally, and smooth the way in every respect. You shall not depose him nor seat anyone of his brothers, elder or younger, on the throne of Assyria instead of him. You shall neither change nor alter the word of Esarhaddon, king of Assyria, but serve this very Assurbanipal, the great crown prince designate, whom Esarhaddon, king of Assyria, your lord, has presented to you, and he shall exercise the kingship and dominion over you.[27]

It is the longest treaty known from Assyria and a complete translation runs to many pages. The text makes it clear that the terms applied not just to those who swore them but also to future generations. And if anybody thought to break their word, alter the text or

The Succession Treaty of Esarhaddon with seal impressions, Kalhu, 672 BC.

destroy their copy of the tablet, they would fall victim to 68 curses listed at the end of the document, a few of which are given here:

> May Assur decree an evil and unpleasant fate for you
> May Anu let disease, exhaustion, malaria, sleeplessness, worries and ill health rain upon all your houses
> May Sin clothe you with leprosy
> May Shamash remove your eyesight
> May Ninurta fill the plain with your blood and feed your flesh to the eagle and vulture
> May Ishtar make your wives lie in the lap of your enemy before your eyes
> May all the great gods of heaven and earth who inhabit the universe and are mentioned by name in this tablet, strike you, look at you in anger, uproot you from among the living and curse you grimly with a painful curse.[28]

To provide the document with divine protection, every tablet was impressed – before the text was written – with three very special cylinder seals. These belonged to the god Assur, as is evident from a caption written at the top of the tablets: 'Seal of the god Assur, king of the gods, lord of the lands – not to be altered; seal of the great ruler, father of the gods – not to be disputed.'[29]

Remarkably, each seal dates to a key period of Assyrian history: the nineteenth, thirteenth and seventh centuries BC. The latest seal, from the time of Sennacherib, is identified by an inscription as Assur's 'Seal of Destinies', thereby associating the treaty with the mythological 'Tablet of Destinies' on which the fate of the cosmos was written.[30]

The text ends with the date and the nature of the document: 'The treaty which Esarhaddon, king of Assyria, concluded on behalf of Assurbanipal, the great crown prince designate of Assyria, and Shamash-shumu-ukin, crown prince designate of Babylon.'[31] If the message wasn't hammered home sufficiently by the oath-taking ceremony, Esarhaddon commissioned a number of monuments that served to underline the new arrangement. Three monumental stelae survive – one from Sam'al (modern Zincirli in Turkey's Gaziantep Province) and two from Til-Barsip (modern Tel Ahmar, on the Euphrates in Syria) – depicting Esarhaddon raising a cone, perhaps containing perfumed oil, to his nose in a religious gesture towards images and symbols of the supreme Assyrian gods. At his feet are miniature figures of the king of Tyre and Taharqa's son (who had been captured in Memphis). Esarhaddon holds in his left hand a mace of authority and the coiled ends of leashes that are attached by rings to the two men's lips. The Assyrian king is not, however, alone in his triumph, as carved on the sides of the stela are the figures of Assurbanipal, facing Esarhaddon and wearing the diadem of the crown prince, and, at the rear of the monarch, Shamash-shumu-ukin.

This effort to ensure a smooth succession, however, seems to have played out against a backdrop of growing discontent among some senior officials, including a few who may have been distant members of the royal family. A number of letters point to conspiracies and attempted rebellions in Nineveh and Ashur. Another plot, perhaps connected with these uprisings, was uncovered by Esarhaddon's agents in Harran (near Urfa in Turkey) in support of a certain Sasi. The conspiracy was even said to have had the blessing of the gods as a slave girl delivered a prophesy: 'This is the word of the god Nusku: Kingship belongs to Sasi. I shall destroy the name and the seed of Sennacherib.'[32] Esarhaddon gathered intelligence about these threats; then, in 670 BC, there was another mass execution of officials. The following year the Assyrian king died (en route to crush the restoration of Taharqa in Egypt) and Assurbanipal (668–*c.* 630 BC) ascended the throne, apparently without opposition. After a period of bloodshed and conspiracy, this may have been viewed as a moment marking a new beginning of peace and prosperity. But, as we will discover, this was the calm before a storm.

Stela of Esarhaddon, Sam'al (Zincirli, Turkey), *c.* 670 BC.

The queen and princesses

> Monument of Sammu-ramat, the palace woman of Shamshi-Adad [V], king of the universe, king of Assyria, mother of Adad-nirari [III], king of the universe, king of Assyria, daughter-in-law of Shalmaneser [III], king of the four quarters.[33]

The most important woman in Assyria was undoubtedly the queen. Her title was *segallu*, literally 'woman of the palace', but she was not simply the wife of the king; in fact, she might not even be his wife. The Assyrian queen was a powerful member of the royal court, the head of an important government office that closely paralleled that of the king – if he was Assur's representative on earth, the queen reflected the goddesses of heaven and she therefore played a major religious role. As one might expect, the position of queen came with enormous wealth: she received tribute and sumptuous audience gifts, just like the king, and managed her own private estates with large numbers of workers engaged in agriculture and manufacture. It should not, therefore, come as a surprise to learn that a treasurer was among the queen's personal staff.

The fact that the queen does not appear in the palace reliefs, at least not until late in the history of the empire, should not lead us to conclude that royal women were in some sense secluded. These carved images were designed to show the male ruler's specific duties in restoring and maintaining divine order through his actions; the queen had other responsibilities but these were probably no less visible to the court and wider population than those of the king. We can begin to appreciate some of her roles from the early ninth century BC, when Queen Mullissu-mukannishat-Ninua took up residence in the newly completed Northwest Palace at Kalhu. She had an extensive household and even her own throne room within a suite of palace apartments. Inscriptions give her full title as 'queen of Assurnasirpal, king of Assyria, and Shalmaneser, king of Assyria ... Daughter of Assur-nirka-da'in, great cupbearer of Assurnasirpal, king of Assyria'.[34] This suggests that Mullissu-mukannishat-Ninua continued as queen even after her husband had been succeeded by Shalmaneser III. This in itself would not have been viewed as unusual as it was up to the new monarch either to allow the office holder to stay in post or to replace her with his own queen. It is possible that Mullissu-mukannishat-Ninua was Shalmaneser's mother, which may have certainly helped her to keep the position, but an immediate family relationship between the queen and the crown prince wasn't a given; the king could have children with different women and then decide to appoint a son as his heir from among them.

Occasionally, circumstances would allow a queen to gain particular prominence, not least when an especially able individual occupied the position. This certainly appears to have been the case with the wife and queen of Shamshi-Adad V: a remarkable woman called Sammu-ramat.[35] On the death of her husband, she continued in office under her son Adad-nirari III, perhaps acting as regent for the young man. When he was of an age to lead a military campaign, Sammu-ramat accompanied him and together they led an Assyrian army across the Euphrates to defeat a local king.[36] Equally unusually, she had her own stela set up at Ashur among those erected for kings and high officials. Her high status is also shown by the inscription on two identical stone statues erected in the temple of the god Nabu at Kalhu. Standing with their hands folded, the bearded figures wear a headdress with bulls' horns, indicating that we are looking at gods, albeit minor ones in the service of Nabu. The statues were commissioned and dedicated by the governor of Kalhu 'for the life of Adad-nirari, king of Assyria, his lord, and for the life of Sammu-ramat, the queen, his lady'.[37]

The most spectacular evidence for Assyrian queens comes from vaulted crypts in the Northwest Palace at Kalhu where some of these powerful women were buried. The purpose-built tombs beneath the palace floors were accessed by means of a shaft and a steep stair to an antechamber that led, through a stone door, into a main chamber where the queen's stone sarcophagus was placed. One of the tombs had a large sarcophagus set into the chamber floor and covered by a heavy stone lid – its size and weight mean that it must have been installed before the construction of the vault and the floor above. Iraqi archaeologists found only a few fragments of bones inside the sarcophagus but its owner could be identified from an inscription carved on the lid; it was the burial place of Mullissu-mukannishat-Ninua. This gave her title as queen of Assurnasirpal II and Shalmaneser III and continued,

> No one later may place here anyone else, whether a palace lady or a queen, nor remove this sarcophagus from its place. Whosoever removes the sarcophagus from its place, his spirit will not receive the funerary offerings with the other spirits. It is a taboo of Shamash [the sun god] and Erishkigal [queen of the underworld]![38]

This text highlights that the queen could expect *kispu* funerary offerings of food and drink to care for her spirit just as for deceased kings. Despite the written curse, however, the tomb was at some point robbed, leaving little for the archaeologists to find in the main chamber. The contents of the antechamber, however, were very different. In this smaller space had been placed three bronze coffins that contained the bodies of at least thirteen women and children, presumably members of the royal family and probably interred over a period of time. Associated with them were over four hundred remarkable objects, including solid gold vessels as well as jewellery and seals of precious stones.[39] Perhaps the most magnificent item is a delicate crown formed from bands of alternating gold pomegranates and rosettes and from which hang delicate clusters of lapis lazuli beads representing grapes. Supporting the top of the crown, which is shaped from gold vine leaves with curling tendrils, are gold winged goddesses shown frontally.

Another vaulted tomb contained a stone sarcophagus with the body of Yaba, wife and queen of Tiglath-pileser III. A stone tablet, set into a niche in the wall of the main chamber, is inscribed with the royal curse on future queens and concubines who might usurp the space:

> Whomever, in the future, be it a queen who sits on the throne or a palace lady who is a concubine of the king, removes me from my tomb, or puts anybody else with me, and lays his hand

Crown of gold and lapis lazuli, possibly of Queen Hama, wife of Shalmaneser IV, Kalhu, *c.* 775 BC.

> upon my jewellery with evil intent or breaks open the seal of that tomb, above (earth), under the rays of the sun, let his spirit roam outside in thirst, below in the underworld, when libations of water are offered, he must not receive with the Anunnaki [gods of the underworld] as a funerary offering any beer, wine or meal. May Ningishzida [god of the underworld] and the great door-keeper, Bitu, the great gods of the underworld, afflict his corpse and ghost with eternal restlessness![40]

When Yaba died, around 35 years of age, she was buried with exquisite funerary goods. Many of these objects were inscribed in cuneiform with the name of their owner and, while some did indeed belong to Yaba, others were marked as the property of Baniti, queen of Shalmaneser V, and Atalia, queen of Sargon II. As both Yaba (the name is in a Semitic dialect spoken in the west of the empire) and Baniti (an Assyrian name) mean 'the beautiful one', it is likely that they refer to the same queen;[41] she must have continued in office under Shalmaneser V. Among her objects is an impressive golden bowl inscribed for Baniti. It was probably used for drinking wine and such vessels are shown being held by the king (and occasionally the queen) on palace wall reliefs and carved ivories depicting banquets. Such bowls are shown being balanced on the tips of the fingers, which might have formed part of formal protocols around dining at court.

But what about Atalia? Surprisingly, the sarcophagus contained the remains of two bodies (in spite of Yaba's curse). The one at the bottom of the coffin is probably that of Yaba and the one laid to rest on top of her is likely to be Atalia. Although queen under Sargon II, Atalia may have died during the reign of his successor, Sennacherib, when she no longer held the position – and was therefore not entitled to a new tomb. She was therefore placed in Yaba/Baniti's sarcophagus along with objects inscribed from the time when she had been queen. Her body was sufficiently well preserved to show that before burial it had been roasted for some time at between 150 and 250°C (300–500°F); perhaps she had died some distance from the capital and this technique was used to help preserve her body for transport to Kalhu.[42]

Sennacherib's queen was Tashmetu-sharrat. Royal inscriptions record how the king built a palace for 'the queen, my beloved wife, whose features Belet-ili has made perfect above all women'.[43] We might read this as a romantic gesture by a loving king – and that is of course very possible – but equally the text highlights how a

Gold bowl of Queen Baniti, wife of Shalmaneser V, Kalhu, *c.* 725 BC.

queen was understood as a paragon of ideal beauty and power, modelled on Assyria's great female deities Mullissu, wife of Assur, and Ishtar, goddess of sexuality and battle.[44] The relationship between these goddesses and the queen becomes even more pronounced in the reign of Sennacherib; both the king and queen play roles in rituals and the references to the queen's military units become more frequent.

Although the precise order of events is rather unclear, Tashmetu-sharrat may have died or been deposed as struggles broke out among Sennacherib's sons to be named crown prince. Esarhaddon's mother was Naqi'a – her name is West Semitic but she was also known by the Assyrian version, Zakutu – and she now rose to prominence and may have been appointed queen before her son ascended the throne in 681 BC; despite a lack of evidence, it is not impossible that she was implicated in Sennacherib's murder. Although Esarhaddon's wife Esharra-hammat was titled queen until her death in 673 BC, Naqi'a may have acted as the head of the queen's household. Very unusually, she was also depicted in sculptures alongside the king, probably participating in rituals with him; a letter refers to a 200-kilogram (440 lb) gold statue of the pair that was to be erected at Kalhu,[45] and Naqi'a appears in relief on a surviving fragment of a bronze sheet, shown at the rear of Esarhaddon. Both hold a cone in their right hand to their nose but the king holds a staff in his left hand while Naqi'a carries a mirror, which had been a symbol of queenship in Assyria for centuries.

Her status was such that when Assurbanipal succeeded to the throne, Naqi'a issued an order under her Assyrian name Zakutu that the whole Assyrian nation swear fealty to him:

> Anyone who is included in this treaty which Queen Zakutu has concluded with the whole nation concerning her favourite grandson Assurbanipal, anyone of you who should fabricate and carry out an ugly and evil thing or a revolt against your lord Assurbanipal, king of Assyria, in your hearts conceive and put words or an ugly scheme or an evil plot against your lord Assurbanipal, king of Assyria . . . and if you hear and know that there are men instigating armed rebellion or fomenting

Hammered bronze sheet showing Esarhaddon and Naqi'a, without provenance, *c.* 680–670 BC.

> conspiracy in your midst, be they bearded or eunuchs or his brothers or of royal life or your brothers or friends or anyone in the entire nation – should you hear and know this, you shall seize and kill them and bring them to Zakutu his [grand] mother and to Assurbanipal, king of Assyria, your lord.[46]

As tradition allowed, however, Assurbanipal chose not to retain his grandmother as queen (although it is also possible that she died soon after he became king), and his wife Libbali-sharrat was installed in the role. It is clear that she had been married to Assurbanipal when he was crown prince from a surviving letter sent by

Detail of the 'Garden Party' relief showing Queen Libbali-sharrat, Nineveh, *c.* 650 BC.

her sister-in-law Sheru'a-etirat (which clearly reveals that members of the royal family were trained to read and write):

> Word of the king's daughter to Libbali-sharrat.
>
> Why don't you write your tablet and do your homework? For if you don't, they will say: 'Is this the sister of Sheru'a-etirat, the eldest daughter of the Succession Palace of Esarhaddon, the great king, mighty king, king of the world, king of Assyria?'
>
> Yet you are only a daughter-in-law – the lady of the house of Assurbanipal, the great crown prince designate of Esarhaddon, king of Assyria![47]

Like Naqi'a before her, Libbali-sharrat appears in sculptures: she has a stela at Ashur and sits enthroned facing the king on the famous 'Garden Party' relief from Assurbanipal's North Palace that we will look at in more detail later. The queen wears the so-called mural crown, which imitates the crenellated walls of Nineveh, and like the mirror is a symbol of Assyrian queenship that can be traced back to (or is a revival of) images of the late second millennium BC.

The role of queen was fundamental in the structure of power in the Assyrian state; together with the king and crown prince they represented on earth the divine family in heaven: Assur, Mullissu and Nabu/Ninurta. But this shouldn't obscure the important roles played by the royal princesses, especially in securing diplomatic alliances through marriage. So, for example, Ahat-abisha, the daughter of Sargon II, was married to a certain prince Ambaris, whose kingdom was located in central Turkey (in the region of modern Kayseri). The aim of the union was to help establish a friendly buffer between Assyrian territories and the powerful states of Phrygia (in central Turkey) and Urartu. In 713 BC, however, Ambaris chose to ally with both of them. The result feels rather predictable from our viewpoint; Sargon sent in troops against Ambaris and the treacherous son-in-law was captured and brought to Assyria in chains, though one might imagine Ahat-abisha was treated more leniently. Such marriages clearly needed careful consideration. Other Assyrian princesses, however, had it easier since their royal husbands were already in Assyria. A legal text of 692 BC makes reference to the 'king's son-in-law' Shoshenq.[48] His North African name suggests that he may have been in Nineveh as a royal hostage, a prince living at court and possibly being groomed as a future pro-Assyrian ruler following Sennacherib's defeat of Egyptian forces during his 701 BC campaign along the east Mediterranean coast, a story for a little later.

The Great Ones

> I [Tiglath-pileser III] annexed those areas to Assyria and placed a eunuch of mine as provincial governor over them . . . I united them, considered them as inhabitants of Assyria, and imposed the yoke of Assur, my lord, upon them as Assyrians.[49]

Until the ninth century BC, the Assyrian king had traditionally delegated authority to men who had inherited their positions by virtue of belonging to ancient noble families. The system was challenged by Assurnasirpal's establishment of Kalhu, when the most senior positions in the Assyrian state were awarded to the ruling king's loyalists but could also be based on merit rather than through family ties. This helped to ensure the monarch's personal security, as well as developing an increased level of professionalism among his advisers and administrators. As Assyrian territory expanded through conquest, this body of men grew in number until there were around one hundred individuals who formed the king's most senior and trusted officials, the so-called Great Ones.[50] Of these, the highest offices of state were the commander-in-chief, treasurer, chief cup-bearer, chief eunuch, palace herald, vizier and chief judge. Many of the Great Ones were eunuchs – that is, castrated men – and this helped to ensure their loyalty to the king since they were unable to father children who might inherit their position and authority and so come to challenge the ruling family. These officials might even take on new names, symbolically giving up their biological family so that they were in some sense adopted by the king as their father. In the reliefs at Kalhu eunuchs appear in close association with the king, undertaking his ritual purification or standing in attendance during audiences and celebrations. One of the most senior courtiers in such scenes can be identified by a long, fringed strip of cloth hanging over his left shoulder. The cloth may have served a ritual purpose, perhaps to wipe the bowl from which the king drank. By the later eighth century BC, this attendant is shown without the shoulder cloth, but now stands with a folded napkin in his left hand and a feather fan in his right hand.[51]

In addition to attending state ceremonies, these officials were appointed at the king's discretion to the most important administrative positions, one of the most significant being governor of an Assyrian province. Until the eighth century BC, the most prestigious roles were to administer territory in the heartland of Assyria, but this began to be transformed with the conquests of Tiglath-pileser III. His successful military challenge to the expanding authority of Urartu from 744 BC resulted in his annexation of vassal states, some of which had been threatening to ally with the northern kingdom, and their reorganization as Assyrian provinces. This offered new, challenging and lucrative opportunities for the king's officials, and by the reign of Sargon II just over twenty years later the governorship over a central Assyrian province was no longer considered the pinnacle of a successful career and instead had become the training ground for running more distant provinces, the latter now considered the most prestigious positions and so held by very experienced and loyal servants of the crown.

As the king's chosen representatives, the governors were all-powerful in their provinces. They were each issued with a gold signet ring bearing a copy of the imperial seal – an image of the king thrusting a sword through a rearing lion. Being in possession of the ring alone would have given the owner the authority of the king, the commands of whom could not be challenged. The same applied to any documents sealed with the ring. Many clay impressions of such seals survive and show slight differences between them in size and design, suggesting that several hundred examples were in use at any one time. They were pressed into clay tablets, but also into clay tags attached to containers and wooden or ivory writing boards. The example here dates to the ninth century BC and the reign of

Senior official with long shoulder cloth standing before Ashurnasirpal II, Kalhu, *c.* 870 BC.

Shalmaneser III. A similar system using rings with their own distinct designs operated for the households of the queen and the crown prince, as well as the governors.[52]

Beyond the provinces were states bound to Assyria through loyalty oaths and treaties. As part of these agreements it was usual for an Assyrian official appointed by the king to reside at the local royal court. This individual would not only monitor regional politics and report back to the Assyrian king, but advise his host on a course of action favourable to Assyria; although technically independent, the local ruler would have been under considerable pressure to accept such advice, which may have often been given as a demand. The Assyrian officials acted as their master's eyes and ears and the information they gathered, along with that of a wide network of agents and informers, flowed back to Kalhu, Dur-Sharrukin or Nineveh. To enable the rapid transfer of intelligence, state officials relied on a system of royal roads along which envoys and letters could be rapidly transported.[53] Known as the 'King's Road', this network of tracks was served by small settlements, effectively way stations, built at strategic locations to provide the travellers with lodging and supplies for the journey. These hamlets served only state officials; they were not available to merchants and

Impression of imperial seal of Shalmaneser III, Kalhu, *c.* 850 BC.

their maintenance fell to the governors in whose provinces they lay. The most important aspect of this imperial communication system was the use of mules for transport. The offspring of a horse mother and a donkey father, mules are strong, fast animals with a longer working life of up to twenty years. A mounted messenger travelled with a second mule as a back-up in case his ride became lame. Sealed letters could be carried in a relay system, being passed to a fresh rider at each station so that there was no delay. In this way information could cross the length of the empire in a matter of days, an Assyrian innovation that transformed the ability to govern imperial territories that came to reach from Egypt to Iran.

This flow of information was dependent on the fact that not only could the royal family and the Great Ones and their deputies read and write cuneiform, but there was an extensive network across the empire of literate officials. These people ranged from the king's secretary, a powerful individual responsible for the royal correspondence, down through different levels and abilities of administrators and functionaries who may have all shared the title of 'scribe' (*tupsharru*). For official correspondence they used the Assyrian dialect of Akkadian that was written in cuneiform on clay tablets; wax-covered writing boards were also used but as these were made from perishable materials such as wood and ivory, few have survived.

As the empire expanded it naturally incorporated regions where other languages were spoken. This wasn't in itself an issue as cuneiform is a flexible script – from its earliest use to write Sumerian, it was adapted to record Semitic Akkadian and later still to write non-Semitic languages of the wider region, such as Hittite and Elamite. There was little challenge, therefore, to integrate people from western Syria and the Levant into the empire given that they spoke Semitic languages such as Hebrew and Aramaic. Local alphabetic systems were, however, in use to record these languages, and as the scripts consisted of just 22 characters written using ink on parchment and papyrus this made an attractive option for administrators as they were much easier to master than cuneiform. A letter from Sargon makes it very clear, however, that this was not appropriate for state correspondence:

> As to what you [the official Sin-iddina] wrote: 'if it is acceptable to the king, let me write and send my messages to the king on Aramaic parchment sheets' – why would you not write and send me [Sargon II] messages in Akkadian? Really, the message which you write in it must be drawn up in this very manner – this is a fixed regulation![54]

Nevertheless, by his reign Aramaic was becoming a language commonly spoken across the empire. This was no doubt being encouraged by the Assyrian practice, described below, of moving populations in large numbers around the Middle East, but the ease with which Aramaic could be written in ink must have also played a role. Documents from Kalhu reveal that Aramaean scribes were already present at the Assyrian court by the early eighth century BC, suggesting that this was increasingly a multilingual world in which officials moved between languages and scripts depending on context. This is made explicit in a palace relief of Tiglath-pileser III that shows a pair of scribes recording the booty from a successful military campaign, including families and their flocks, the details of which are being dictated to them by a senior official. One scribe holds a rectangular tablet in his left hand and a cuneiform stylus in the other. His companion, however, uses a pen to write on a leather roll. Unlike clay, leather parchment is a very fragile material and no examples of such documents have survived from Assyria. It seems certain, however, that the administrative archives and royal libraries of the empire contained vast numbers of scrolls alongside the thousands of clay tablets that recorded the day-to-day operation of the state but also the crucial knowledge generated and used by the king's greatest scholars, some of whom we will encounter a little later.

The army, warfare and brutality

> I [Sargon II] mustered the numerous troops of the god Assur and marched to conquer those cities. I shattered their very strong walls with a mighty battering ram, levelling them to the ground. I carried off as booty

Relief showing Assyrian scribes recording details on a cuneiform tablet and a leather roll, Kalhu, *c.* 730 BC.

> the people, together with their property. I destroyed, demolished, and burned down those cities with fire.[55]

The ninth century BC was a period of enormous transformation for the Assyrian state and this was especially true for its military. What had comprised an infantry of seasonally conscripted farmers along with a chariotry led by the nobility started to grow into a permanent professionalized standing army. A significant development was in the use of horses. Since at least the mid-second millennium BC, a fundamental component of armies on the plains of Mesopotamia and Syria was light chariots pulled by one or two pairs of horses. This vehicle takes centre stage in the scenes of battle on the throne room reliefs from Kalhu, with Assurnasirpal II leading the charge against his enemies, accompanied by a second chariot containing a tall standard surmounted by an image of a god. The king is shown using his bow and he is joined in the chariot cab by a shield bearer, who protects him from incoming arrows, and a chariot driver holding the reins. This is a high-prestige, expensive vehicle and would be associated with the king in his role as warrior in Assyrian texts and art until the very end of the empire. But the Kalhu images also show some of the earliest examples of a change in the use of horses in battle, with the appearance among the Assyrian forces of a pair of cavalrymen who fight alongside each other using the same arrangement as in a chariot: one rider is an archer using a bow, the other holds a shield and the reins of both horses. They pursue fleeing horsemen and it was these mobile riders who provided the key to the eventual development and expansion in the use of Assyrian cavalry.[56]

The strength of the army was therefore dependent on the regular supply of horses and so a strategic goal of every Assyrian king was to gain control of the horse-breeding communities in the mountains to the north and east of Assyria. Campaigns were launched to acquire animals either as plunder or as tribute and, when territories were incorporated into the state, through taxation. Chariot warfare was impractical in such rugged landscapes – the vehicles needed to be dismantled and carried – and this helped to drive the change towards mounted warriors. These same military campaigns also provided Assyria with another crucial resource for its army only available in the highlands – iron ore for the production of swords, spears and arrowheads.

Assurnasirpal II in his war chariot, Kalhu, *c.* 870 BC.

Alongside the chariotry and cavalry, the regular infantry consisted of archers fighting together with or without shield bearers and spearmen. Pitched open battles involved thousands of soldiers: Assurnasirpal II boasts of some 50,000 men. The palace reliefs show them engaged in close-combat fighting with shields and swords. They were also, of course, crucial in the storming of settlements, but also prepared the way for such attacks by acting as sappers or as tunnellers to undermine defensive walls. Sieges could involve the use of battering rams and towers on wheels that would bring the archers closer to the enemy battlements.[57]

The royal inscriptions and carved images devote considerable space to descriptions of the capture of cities, but in reality this was avoided where possible. It could take months, if not years, to accomplish the siege and capture of large settlements and as a result it was a very expensive undertaking – one that could also lead to famine and disease inside the besieged city. As a result, various methods were used to encourage submission: negotiation with communities and their leaders in which local rights and practices would be guaranteed in exchange for political oversight and taxation; the local communities were encouraged to comply through the distribution of bribes, the destruction of their crops – the felling of orchards was a favoured scene for artists recounting such action – or the public execution of rebel leaders.[58]

As Assyrian territory expanded under Shalmaneser III, soldiers were stationed for extended periods in strategic border regions, while fighters captured on campaign began to be incorporated into the army. By the mid-eighth century BC, large groups of foreign origin were being recruited in the provinces or incorporated into Assyrian service following their defeat in battle.[59] Distinguished on the palace reliefs by their crested helmets, they formed a light infantry composed of archers and spearmen. In the same period Assyrian cavalry units were replacing light chariotry. This transformed the army into a much more professional force with the result that conscripts were unnecessary, which freed military campaigns from being tied to the agricultural seasons so they could take place at different times of the year and much further afield.

The basic unit in the army comprised fifty men led by an officer. The different contingents were allowed to preserve and develop their own customs and identities and competition between them was encouraged for the attention of the king, who would offer rewards and promotion for bravery and success in battle. The monarch was in command of his own royal cohort while other parts of the army were placed under the authority of high officials. When on campaign the troops lived in tents within temporary fortified camps. Here they were supported by a large number of non-combatants, who maintained equipment, cared for the horses and fed the soldiers by foraging for supplies in the surrounding countryside. Although there were permanent garrisons in forts established in strategic border areas, the provinces of the empire had no soldiers stationed within them. Nor did provincial governors control their own troops, except those mobilized in emergencies or brought in from elsewhere; this was a very effective way of ensuring that these senior officials remained dependent for their security on the central authorities and that there was little opportunity for them to develop their own forces that might come to threaten the king. These arrangements also meant that soldiers would have been far less evident to the inhabitants of the empire than was the case with many later imperial powers.

Successful military campaigns – much like successful animal hunts – were marked in Assyria by processions, rituals and feasts.[60] In the Kalhu palace reliefs we see individuals dressed in the skins of lions, while Assyrian soldiers appear to play catch with the severed heads of enemies. The king and the standard of the gods are welcomed back to the capital by the palace women, who stand on the crenellated walls of the palace and clap in celebration. The prisoners and booty were then paraded before the king, accompanied by music. By the seventh century BC, such moments had been transformed into huge public events. Celebrations also included elaborate banquets. As we have seen, the western suite of rooms in the Northwest Palace was likely intended for such affairs. Such communal feasting, at least among Assyria's nobility, is represented in many reliefs from Sargon II's palace at Dur-Sharrukin. Here we see not only the event itself but the preparations, with courtiers

Auxiliary troops of Sennacherib, Nineveh, *c.* 690 BC.

carrying tables, chairs and drinking cups in the form of small buckets in the shape of lion heads. Scenes of banqueting show men raising their cups – whether these were formal, choreographed occasions or more rowdy drunken affairs is unclear; perhaps the former turned into the latter as time progressed.

Triumph in battle was also the moment to humiliate and punish those who had defied Assur and his earthly king. While victory in battle was achieved through the support of the gods, as time passed the royal inscriptions and images increasingly shift the focus from generic statements of warfare and success towards narratives around specific historical events that highlight particular rebel people and their leaders. By the time of Assurbanipal in the mid-seventh century BC, the scribes and artists at Nineveh were creating very detailed – and to our thinking very gory – accounts of the torture and execution of named individuals, presenting their actions as very personal attacks on the king as well as the gods. Modern viewers of such scenes have often assumed that Assyrian society revelled in such cruelty, but the images are little different in content to, say, those depicting state executions under Renaissance England's Henry VIII when political and religious opponents of the king were condemned to be either burnt alive, beheaded or 'hung, drawn and quartered' – in other words, chopped up – all taking place within the context of an otherwise magnificent court. So, for example, we can read in Assurbanipal's accounts,

Assyrian soldiers at victory celebrations, Kalhu, *c.* 870 BC.

> As for Mannu-ki-ahhe . . . who had uttered grievous blasphemies against my gods, I ripped out their tongues and flayed them inside the city of Arbela.
>
> As for the rest of the brothers . . . I killed them, chopped up their flesh and sent them out to be a spectacle in all the lands.
>
> As for Nabu-na'id and Bel-etir, sons of Nabu-shuma-eresh, the governor of Nippur, whose father had stirred up Urtaku to fight with the land of Babylonia – the bones of Nabu-Shuma-eresh, which they had taken out of the land of Gambulu to Assyria, I made them crush those bones opposite the Citadel Gate of Nineveh.[61]

Such descriptions were intended to mark the fulfilment of a just punishment and the restoration of peace and order as demanded by the gods. It finds parallels in the royal hunt, especially the death of dangerous animals such as lions, as will be described in a later section.

The four quarters of the world

> Palace of Tiglath-pileser [III], great king, mighty king,
> king of the world, king of Assyria, king of Babylon, king
> of Sumer and Akkad, king of the four quarters of the world;
> valiant man who, with the help of Assur, his lord, smashed
> like pots all who were unsubmissive to him.[62]

The forty years between the accession of Tiglath-pileser III in 745 BC and the death of Sargon II in 705 BC were transformative for Assyria. The incorporation of conquered territory as directly governed provinces allowed Assyrian monarchs to claim, with some justification, the ancient royal title of 'king of the four quarters of the world', indicating their control over territories in all directions. Let us take a tour around the edges of the emerging empire to explore some of the key regions and the challenges they brought to Assyria.

Urartu

The bronze winged human-headed bull with a missing face was most likely part of an elaborate throne. It dates to the late eighth century BC and comes from the Urartian site of Toprakkale, near Lake Van in eastern Turkey. The face may have been of ivory or white stone, as is known from other figures; the wings would have been inlaid and the whole would have been gilded. The bull would have been accompanied on the throne by other figures such as winged lions, griffins, gods in human form standing on the backs of bulls, and human attendants. It is possible that they served to support the arms of the throne, intended to magically protect the individual who used it. This may have been a king, certainly an important official of one of Assyria's most powerful adversaries.

The kingdom of Urartu dominated the rugged, mountainous region lying to the north of Assyria between and around the three great lakes of Van, Urmia (in northwestern Iran) and Sevan (in Armenia).[63] This was a region with two key resources coveted by the Assyrian state: metals, especially copper, and horses. As early as the thirteenth century BC, Assyrian kings had conducted raids into the area, which in their inscriptions is named the 'land of Nairi'. These texts suggest that the region was divided among a number of small states, with those around Lake Van being a particular focus. By the ninth century BC, however, as Assurnasirpal II and Shalmaneser III consolidated control over northern Mesopotamia, Urartu had emerged as a single kingdom, possibly unified in response to Assyrian aggression. The earliest known Urartian written document dates to this period. It is a rock inscription at the Urartian capital, Turushpa, which was located on the eastern shore of Lake Van on a high rock outcrop. It names the Urartian ruler Sarduri (*c.* 840–830 BC), as well as his supreme god, Haldi. The king was expanding Urartu's authority northwards into the Caucasus and eastwards into northwest Iran. Probably taking its lead from Assyria, the Urartian royal court adopted cuneiform and Sarduri's inscription is written in the Assyrian language. From the time of his son and successor Ishpuini (*c.* 830–810 BC) onwards, however, Urartian (which is related to the earlier Hurrian language) was recorded.

Bronze human-headed winged bull, part of a throne, Toprakkale, Turkey, c. 750–700 BC.

In the first half of the eighth century BC, Urartu took advantage of a weakened Assyria and sought to extend its influence over north Syria and southern Anatolia. A Urartian army defeated the forces of Assur-nirari V (754–745 BC) in the territory of the north Syrian kingdom of Arpad, which had formerly accepted Assyria as its overlord. The defeat may have led to a crisis at the Assyrian court that brought Tiglath-pileser III to the throne. The new Assyrian king sought to reverse Assyria's declining authority by going on the offensive, and in 743 BC he defeated the Urartian army in a battle in Arpad (centred on modern Tell Rifaat, north of Aleppo in northwest Syria), and drove it back to Turushpa. This would be the only time when Assyrian troops ever reached the Urartian capital.

The balance of power had shifted and Urartu may have appeared contained, but the northern kingdom now turned its focus on winning over a number of states located in northwestern Iran. Several of these were on Assyria's borders following Tiglath-pileser's establishment of several provinces in the region. As a result Sargon II was forced to fight a series of wars against these states. Among them was Musasir, which was under increasing pressure from Assyria to cut its ties with Urartu. The kingdom contained an immensely important – and extremely wealthy – temple dedicated to the god Haldi that was the destination of an annual pilgrimage by the Urartian royal court. In 714 BC, as part of a longer campaign to crush Urartian influence in northwest Iran, Sargon led a successful raid against Musasir in which the temple was sacked, providing the Assyrian king with an enormous windfall which he invested in the creation of his new capital city, Dur-Sharrukin.

The Medes

To the east of Assyria lay the mountain valleys of the Zagros that were home to a people of whom some were identified by the Assyrians as Medes, perhaps because they shared a common language and culture focused on the rearing of cattle and horses. The region was divided between a number of 'city lords' who controlled territory from fortresses that dominated overland trade routes, not least the Great Khorasan Road – part of what today we think of as the 'Silk Road' – which linked lowland Mesopotamia with the highlands of Iran. The wealth of the city lords was derived from taxation and offering protection at a price to merchants and other travellers passing along these roads. The Median settlements also supplied manufactured goods such as metal objects and rugs as well as animals and their products. Control of the resources that flowed along these trade arteries was important for Assyria, and in 744 BC Tiglath-pileser III established by force of arms two provinces in

Median territory: one at the headwaters of the Diyala river, and another further to the east in the Zagros Mountains.[64] As a result, Assyria came to directly control a section of the Great Khorasan Road and so secured the army's horse supplies.

Babylonia

Babylonia represented a special case for the Assyrians. A vast land of alluvial plains and marshy delta that was divided between ancient cities – with renowned temples and seats of learning – and tribal regions, the political landscape was one of ever-changing relations and loyalties, a shifting maze that mirrored the natural and artificial watercourses that criss-crossed the country. The great city of Babylon, cult centre of the god Marduk, was no longer the prime centre of political authority it had once been, but nevertheless retained its symbolic value as the seat of the Babylonian king even if in practice other cities such as Uruk and Nippur managed their own affairs. These large urban centres had populations that included members of Aramaean and Chaldean tribal groups who identified themselves as belonging to 'houses' (*bit*). The most powerful and wealthy were Bit-Yakin, Bit-Dakkuri and Bit-Amukani, who controlled the extensive pasturelands and marshes between cities, as well as the river courses and ports. As we have explored, from the middle of the second millennium BC relations between Assyria and Babylonia moved between friendship (and royal marriage alliances) to military confrontation, not least at the borders and in the region east of the river Tigris. Tiglath-pileser III led his forces into this politically fragmented region in support of pro-Assyrian factions. His authority was increasingly being challenged by a powerful rival, Mukin-zeri, chief of the Bit-Amukani, who, in attempting to unify Babylonia behind him, claimed the throne of Babylon in 731 BC. The Assyrian army moved against Mukin-zeri and ultimately defeated him, with Tiglath-pileser III taking the crown of Babylon for himself in 729 BC. For the remainder of his reign, he ruled as both the king of Assyria and the king of Babylonia. Holding the southern kingdom's throne would, however, prove challenging for his successors, not least as the anti-Assyrian cities and tribes would seek support from Babylonia's neighbours, especially the kingdom of Elam in southeast Iran.

Elam

Elam was a very ancient kingdom that may have existed as early as the late fourth millennium BC. It brought together politically the highland city of Anshan with that of Susa, which lay at the edge of an extension of the Babylonian alluvium.[65] Although Elam had been one of the great powers of the Middle East in the second millennium BC, controlling the flow of tin and other highland resources towards trading cities like Ashur and occasionally dominating cities in Babylonia, its widespread influence had declined. By the start of the first millennium BC, Persian tribal groups had entered the region as, further north along the eastern flanks of the Zagros Mountains, other Iranian-speaking peoples, the Medes, consolidated their presence. By the mid-eighth century BC, Susa was no longer the main city of Elam and Assyrian texts name Madaktu and Hudalu as the political centres of a fragmented and unstable region yet one sufficiently powerful to be a major obstacle to Assyrian control over the east Tigris and Babylonia.

Egypt and Kush

At the start of the eighth century BC, Egypt was divided among a number of rulers in the Nile Delta, many of Libyan origin, while the Nile valley to the south (Upper Egypt) was under the control of the city of Thebes as far as the first cataract (an unnavigable stretch of rocky outcrops at Aswan). From here on south the valley was dominated by the kingdom of Kush, which was centred on the city of Napata at Jebel Barkal in modern-day Sudan.[66] During the second millennium BC this extensive region – which provided accesses to the rich resources of Africa, not least gold – had been dominated by Egypt. However, although cultural ties had remained close, by 1000 BC Kush was independent and unified under local rulers. Around 750 BC King Kashta of Kush took advantage of Egypt's internal instability and expanded his authority over Thebes. His successor, Piye (747–714 BC), launched a military campaign through Egypt, possibly in response to the growing power of rulers in the north of the country. Memphis resisted but eventually submitted, and with the other delta dynasts recognized Piye as their overlord. The Kushite king was content to leave most subjugated local rulers in place and it was left to his successor Shabako (*c.* 713–700 BC) to formally annex Egypt to Kush. Adopting the ambition of earlier pharaohs, the new rulers of Egypt now looked to reinstate the country's historic political and military dominance in the Levant, with the result that many kingdoms in the region sought alliances against the expansionist ambitions of their neighbours and increasingly Assyria. During the reigns of Tiglath-pileser III, Shalmaneser V and Sargon II, relations between Assyria and Kush remained peaceful, but it was perhaps inevitable that the two powers would eventually clash.

Judah, Israel and Damascus

From the eastern Nile Delta a route follows the coast of the Mediterranean Sea across north Sinai into a more hospitable coastal plain. Here the Philistine cities of Gaza, Ashdod and Ekron benefited from trading ports with close connections to Egypt. Inland, behind these small city states, lay the hill country of Judah with its capital at Jerusalem. From both lowland and highland, roads ran northwards to the two most powerful and wealthy kingdoms of the region: Israel and Damascus. Israel had access to sea ports through a wide gap between the hills of Judah and the Lebanon mountain range. This was rich farming land but it was also a strategically and economically important link between the Mediterranean coastal plain and the river Jordan and inland desert routes. Damascus was Israel's eastern neighbour and main rival for control of the overland trade, not least the roadways through Syria to eastern Anatolia and Assyria. Relations between Israel and Damascus wavered between cooperation and hostility, and to some extent these local politics determined their individual relations with Assyria; they either sought alliance with the kings in Kalhu, Dur-Sharrukin and Nineveh or dared to face their wrath.

One of their earliest military encounters with Assyria brought Israel and Damascus together in cooperation. In 853 BC Shalmaneser III crossed the Euphrates with an army intent on plundering the small states of Syria, probably with an aim of reaching the Mediterranean, an achievement that held great symbolic value for Mesopotamian kings. He found his way blocked, however, by a formidable army that had come together at Qarqar on the river Orontes in western Syria. Among the army were Ahaz of Israel and Hadad-ezer of Damascus. The Assyrian king lists the impressive forces arrayed against him, including:

> 1,200 chariots, 1,200 cavalry and 20,000 troops of Hadad-ezer, the Damascene;
> 700 chariots, 700 cavalry and 10,000 troops of lrhulenu, the Hamatite;
> 2,000 chariots and 10,000 troops of Ahab the Israelite;
> 500 troops of Byblos;
> 1,000 troops of Egypt;
> 1,000 camels of Gindibu of the Arabs.[67]

The Assyrian king presents the outcome of the confrontation as his victory, but the fact that he didn't advance any further suggests that Shalmaneser had likely met his match.

Several decades on, however, the new ruler of Israel, Jehu, offered Shalmaneser III an alliance. The importance of this agreement to Assyria – allowing it access to a strategic region – is reflected by the depiction of the Israelite king in a prominent position on the so-called Black Obelisk from Kalhu. The encounter between the two rulers is presented in a central panel on the monument with Jehu shown prostrating himself in submission before Shalmaneser while his gifts paraded before the Assyrian king are described in the accompanying cuneiform caption as 'tribute'. The same text describes Jehu as belonging to Bit-Humri, the 'House of Omri', the name of Israel used by the Assyrian scribes after the kingdom's founder.

From 744 BC Tiglath-pileser III aggressively enforced Assyrian domination over northern Syria, establishing provinces and

reorienting trade and communication routes in his favour. This forced Israel and Damascus to rethink their alliances with northern states now under Assyrian control and they looked instead to the wealthy Phoenician city of Tyre and markets in Egypt. Such relationships were a troubling development for Tiglath-pileser as it offered a chance for Egypt to gain a foothold in the region. In 734 BC, therefore, an Assyrian army campaigned along the Levantine coast, conquering Gaza, which helped to ensure that Egypt was contained. But this action alone was clearly not sufficient as two years later an Assyrian army besieged and captured Damascus, converting its territory into a province. Israel was also attacked and the northern parts of the kingdom, including the city of Megiddo, were taken by the Assyrians and reorganized as a province, with part of the population deported: 'The land of Bit-Humri, all of whose

Detail of the Black Obelisk of Shalmaneser III showing the submission of Jehu of Israel, Kalhu, *c.* 825 BC.

cities I had utterly devastated in my former campaigns, whose people and livestock I had carried off and whose capital city Samaria alone had been spared: now they overthrew Peqah, their king.'[68]

Much reduced in size, Israel was cut off from the sea and Tiglath-pileser installed a new ruler, Hoshea, who would be more amenable to Assyrian interests. These events are also described in the Hebrew Bible but from the perspective of Judah. With the delivery of tribute, King Ahaz of Judah sought an alliance with Tiglath-pileser through which he could expect the growing empire to protect his kingdom from his aggressive northern neighbours:

> Ahaz sent messengers to say to Tiglath-pileser king of Assyria, 'I am your servant and vassal. Come up and save me out of

> the hand of the king of Aram [Damascus] and of the king of Israel, who are attacking me.' And Ahaz took silver and gold . . . and sent it as a gift to the king of Assyria. The king of Assyria complied. (2 Kings 16:7–9)

The arrangement suited Assyria as it established another buffer between its territories and Egypt. Nevertheless, the next biblical verse describes how some years later Israel sought an alliance with 'So, king of Egypt' (2 Kings 17:4), possibly Osorkon IV (730–716 BC). Tiglath-pileser's son and successor, Shalmaneser V, launched an invasion of Israel but it took a three-year-long siege to capture Samaria in 722 BC. This was followed by the deportation of large parts of the population: 'The king of Assyria captured Samaria and deported the Israelites to Assyria. He settled them in Halah [Halahhu in central Assyria], in Gozan [Guzana in northeast Syria] on the Habur river and in the towns of the Medes [in the Zagros Mountains]' (2 Kings 17:6).

Samaria now became the centre of a new Assyrian province. The kingdom of Judah, however, remained independent and proved a loyal ally to Assyria until the death of Sargon II. It, too, then faced the consequences of rebellion against the empire, a story to which we will return.

Phoenicia

A carved ivory panel – one of an almost identical pair – shows an African boy with jewelled armlets and bracelets being attacked by a lioness. Above them is a dense network of lilies and papyrus. Much of the surface of the ivory was once covered with gold leaf and inlaid with carnelian and lapis lazuli. The African wears a short kilt covered in gold leaf and the curls of his hair are marked with gold. A spot of lapis lazuli is inlaid on the forehead of the lioness.

Found at Kalhu, where it had probably arrived as booty or tribute, this remarkable carving may have been part of an elaborate piece of furniture, perhaps a throne, made in one of the wealthy states occupying a narrow strip of land between the sea and the

Lebanon mountain range (the coast of modern Lebanon and Syria). These were the coastal cities of Sidon and Byblos and the island cities of Tyre and Arwad that benefited from natural harbours and were the centres of maritime trade.[69] Although they were independent kingdoms, they shared a language and culture. The Greeks called them Phoenicians, a word also used for both the murex snail and the colour purple extracted from it. Textiles dyed purple were among the luxuries in which the Phoenicians traded, along with glass beads, copper ingots and timber from the cedars of Lebanon – and the Assyrian court was one of their most important clients.

Tyre in particular was connected with Assyria through trading agreements that gave the island city an advantage over other

Carved ivory panel in Phoenician style, Kalhu, *c.* 800 BC.

neighbouring states and in return provided Assyria with taxes and access to supplies of wood and other materials. Such relationships may have also helped to encourage the westward expansion of Phoenician settlements around the Mediterranean, which had been under way since the ninth century. One of the earliest colonies was established by Tyre on the island of Cyprus, prized for its rich copper deposits. The trade networks made the Phoenicians rich – and by association also the Assyrians – but it also led to the spread of Assyrian imagery and ideas into the Mediterranean alongside the Phoenician alphabetic writing system of 22 characters which was widely adopted.

Aramaean and Neo-Hittite states

Coming full circle, we arrive back in northwestern Syria and the Aramaean city state of Arpad, where Tiglath-pileser defeated an Urartian army in 743 BC. He then turned on Arpad itself but it took three years for the Assyrian forces to defeat the kingdom. Having done so, Tiglath-pileser made the radical decision to directly annex it to the Assyrian state, converting the territory into two provinces. Next, he had to deal with Arpad's allies. Hamath on the Orontes was defeated in 738 BC. The conflict dragged on, however, as Hamath had been assisted by Damascus and Israel, which, as we have seen, would also come to be absorbed into the empire. When Hamath fell to Tiglath-pileser, he also conquered its neighbour, Unqi. This was a so-called Neo-Hittite state, one of several kingdoms in north Syria and southeast Turkey that maintained the language and traditions of the long-vanished Hittite Empire and were thus known to the Assyrians as Hatti. One of the wealthiest and most powerful kingdoms of Hatti was Carchemish on the river Euphrates. It would eventually fall to the army of Sargon II in 717 BC following a revolt against Assyrian overlordship – probably with the support of Urartu.

Resistance

> How can a man who has made a revolt against the king [Tiglath-pileser III], my lord, and conspired against the Kingdom, enjoy bread and happiness?[70]

By 700 BC Assyrian authority reached from the Mediterranean coast of Syria and Turkey to the marshlands of southern Iraq and the Persian Gulf. The empire at this point encompassed a geographical area equivalent to roughly that of modern Spain or the U.S. state of California – extensive yet very manageable by a well-organized administration.[71] It was divided beyond the Assyrian heartland into more than forty provinces. As we have seen, key to this structure was the appointment of provincial governors who were representatives of the king and tasked with the management of agricultural production, manufacturing, trade and taxation. Deportations of people from other regions of the empire provided workers as needed. There was very little incentive, and indeed very few opportunities, for opposition to the established order from among the inhabitants of the towns and villages within a province. While there were militarized areas in strategically sensitive regions of the empire, the presence of soldiers was otherwise quite unusual. When trouble did occur, it was often in regions where there were competing political loyalties, a complex, shifting landscape of pro- and anti-Assyrian groupings. We will look at two such examples, kingdoms at opposite ends of the empire and the circumstances that led to periods of resistance to Assyrian authority from Judah (in 701 BC) and Babylonia (in 691–689 BC).

Let us start in the far southwest and the kingdom of Judah, which controlled the hilly country between the Dead Sea and the Mediterranean coastal plain. As trade networks flourished and expanded during the eighth century BC, its capital, Jerusalem, had grown from a small town into a city. The political situation in the region changed dramatically for Judah when its northern neighbour, Israel, was defeated in 722 BC and was transformed into an Assyrian province. Judah was now squeezed between the Assyrian Empire and Egypt, lying to its south and under the control of the

Kushite Dynasty who, as has been noted, were keen to expand their authority along the Mediterranean coast. The political tightrope that Judah's rulers had been carefully walking had become even more precarious. A crisis arose in 701 BC when the Phoenician city of Sidon openly rebelled against Assyria. Neighbouring kingdoms had to choose sides and King Hezekiah of Judah, having been almost certainly assured of support from Egypt, felt emboldened (or cornered) to join the rebel alliance. Other rulers were more hesitant and in the neighbouring state of Ekron the pro-Assyrian king Padi was overthrown and handed to Hezekiah, who imprisoned him in Jerusalem.

These events and what followed can be reconstructed from a unique combination of written sources and carved images, each composed with very different agendas. Although they need to be treated with caution since they were never intended as impartial reporting, some aspects of these accounts can also be confirmed by archaeology. The Assyrian version is provided by the royal inscriptions of Sennacherib from Nineveh. It is paralleled by accounts in the Hebrew Bible.

Sennacherib moved to counter this dangerous situation, which threatened the loss to Assyria of a wealthy city and the trade (and taxes) that flowed from it. Troops were assembled at Nineveh and the king led them towards the Mediterranean, gathering forces as he passed through provinces in Syria, before marching into the territory of Sidon. The rebel ruler of Sidon fled and Sennacherib appointed a new king to replace him. Meanwhile some of the neighbouring states sent sumptuous gifts to the Assyrian monarch. The sequence of events is rather confused but, according to Sennacherib's account, he was victorious in a battle against a Kushite army that had come to the support of the rebellion. The Assyrian king followed up by dealing with members of the resistance:

> I [Sennacherib] approached the city of Ekron and I killed the governors and nobles who had committed crimes and hung their corpses on towers around the city; I counted the citizens who had committed the criminal acts as booty; and I commanded that the rest of them, those who were not guilty

> of crimes or wrongdoing, to whom no penalty was due, be allowed to go free.[72]

An order was issued that Hezekiah should free Padi. Jerusalem had been prepared for attack by the strengthening of the surrounding wall and the digging of a 530-metre (1,750 ft) tunnel so that water of the Gihon spring could be reached from inside the city. To force Hezekiah to submit, Sennacherib therefore launched attacks against other towns in Judah:

> As for Hezekiah of Judah, I surrounded and conquered forty-six of his fortified walled cities and smaller settlements in their environs, which were without number, by having ramps trodden down and battering rams brought up, the assault of foot soldiers, sapping, breaching, and siege engines. I brought out of them 200,150 people, young and old, male and female, horses, mules, donkeys, camels, oxen, and sheep and goats, which were without number, and I counted them as booty.[73]

Beyond Jerusalem one of the most important cities in Judah was Lachish. The Assyrian success in besieging and capturing the fortified settlement is documented in a series of reliefs lining the walls of a room in Sennacherib's palace at Nineveh. The narrative is told in five episodes. On entering the room, a visitor would have seen that the story begins on the left-most panels with the advance of the Assyrian artillery. This comprises slingers with piles of round missiles; then come archers and at the front stormtroopers with shields and spears. Next in the sequence of carved slabs, which was placed directly opposite the entrance door guarded by a pair of *lamassus*, is a view of the towered walls of Lachish itself under attack. Siege engines with battering rams are wheeled up artificial ramps surfaced with planks. Soldiers also move up the ramps in pairs, one shooting arrows while his companion covers them both with a shield. As the attack takes place, time is compressed so that the end is made clear with some of the inhabitants leaving the city gate. In the third episode, the people of Lachish move through the orchards of the town as they are deported to be resettled elsewhere in the empire. Next comes a scene in which men with tightly curled hair and beards – who might be identified as Kushites – are tortured and executed or drop to their knees in submission. Finally, on the right-hand wall of the room, Sennacherib is shown seated on a throne in majesty before his royal pavilion; set on a hill overlooking the ruined city, the king watches the booty of Lachish pass before him.

The storming of the city of Lachish in 701 BC, Nineveh, *c.* 690 BC.

top: Families deported from the city of Lachish, Nineveh, *c.* 690 BC.
bottom: Sennacherib enthroned outside of Lachish, Nineveh, *c.* 690 BC.

This vivid imagery is made very real by the evidence unearthed by archaeologists at the site of Lachish. Here was uncovered an Assyrian siege ramp some 79 metres (260 ft) long and formed from some 20,000 tons of stones.[74] It would have taken hundreds of workers labouring 24 hours a day over three weeks to build the ramp. The surface of the ramp was covered with a stamped layer of dirt and then with wooden boards, just as depicted on the Nineveh reliefs.

According to the biblical account, Sennacherib now sent a delegation with a military force to Jerusalem:

> The king of Assyria sent his supreme commander, his chief officer and his field commander with a large army, from Lachish to King Hezekiah at Jerusalem. They came up to Jerusalem and stopped at the aqueduct of the Upper Pool, on the road to the Washerman's Field. They called for the king; and Eliakim son of Hilkiah the palace administrator, Shebna the secretary, and Joah son of Asaph the recorder went out to them.
>
> The field commander said to them, 'Tell Hezekiah: This is what the great king, the king of Assyria, says: On what are you basing this confidence of yours? You say you have the counsel and the might for war – but you speak only empty words. On whom are you depending, that you rebel against me? Look, I know you are depending on Egypt, that splintered reed of a staff, which pierces the hand of anyone who leans on it! Such is Pharaoh king of Egypt to all who depend on him.' (2 Kings 18:17–21)

This was sufficient to persuade Hezekiah to submit to the Assyrian king, releasing Padi back to Ekron and sending Sennacherib a huge payment as an expression of his loyalty:

> So Hezekiah king of Judah sent this message to the king of Assyria at Lachish: 'I have done wrong. Withdraw from me, and I will pay whatever you demand of me.' The king of Assyria exacted from Hezekiah king of Judah three hundred talents of silver and thirty talents of gold. So Hezekiah gave him all the silver that was found in the temple of the Lord and in the treasuries of the royal palace. At this time Hezekiah king of Judah stripped off the gold with which he had covered the doors and doorposts of the temple of the Lord, and gave it to the king of Assyria. (2 Kings 18:14–16)

Sennacherib's account of his campaign provides an even more impressive list of the payments from Judah:

> As for him, Hezekiah, fear of my lordly brilliance overwhelmed him and, after my departure, he had the auxiliary forces and his elite troops whom he had brought inside to strengthen Jerusalem, his royal city, thereby gaining reinforcements, along with 30 talents of gold, 800 talents of silver, choice antimony . . . ivory beds, armchairs of ivory, elephant hides, elephant ivory, ebony, boxwood, garments with multi-coloured trim, linen garments, blue-purple wool, red-purple wool, utensils of bronze, iron, copper, tin, and iron, chariots, shields, lances, armour, iron belt-daggers, bows and arrows, equipment, and implements of war, all of which were without number, together with his daughters, his palace women, male singers, and female singers brought into Nineveh, my capital city, and he sent a mounted messenger of his to me to deliver this payment and to do obeisance.[75]

This settlement in goods and people had saved Jerusalem from being besieged. For the compilers of the Hebrew Bible such a happy outcome for the city could only be explained through divine intervention and so they offered a dramatic, albeit wishful, finale:

> That night the angel of the Lord went out and put to death a hundred and eighty-five thousand in the Assyrian camp. When the people got up the next morning – there were all the dead bodies! So Sennacherib king of Assyria broke camp and withdrew. He returned to Nineveh and stayed there. (2 Kings 19:35–6)

While Sennacherib's crushing of rebellion in the west of the empire – and successfully confronting Egypt's expansionist aims – was considered worthy of representation on his palace walls at Nineveh, the greatest challenge to Assyrian authority came from the southern kingdom of Babylonia.

To say that the relationship between Assyria and Babylonia was complicated would be an understatement as the two kingdoms had pivoted between alliance and confrontation over many centuries. We can begin this story as we did in the west in the later eighth century. In 729 BC the forces of Tiglath-pileser III conquered Babylonia, making him the first Assyrian king to do so since the triumphs of Tukulti-Ninurta I in the thirteenth century. In the turbulent times following Sargon II's usurpation of the throne in 722 BC, however, a powerful Babylonian tribal leader called Marduk-aplu-iddina of Bit-Yakin exploited the unrest to assume the kingship of Babylon. It took Sargon over a decade to retake the capital city by force, but in 710 BC he reclaimed the throne for Assyria, staying in Babylon for a number of years. After Sargon was killed on campaign, however, Marduk-aplu-iddina returned to be crowned again as the Babylonian king. Now it was the turn of Sennacherib to send Assyrian forces south and, following a series of fierce assaults between 704 and 702 BC, Marduk-aplu-iddina was once again deposed. Sennacherib, however, did not take the throne for himself but installed Bel-ibni, a member of an old family from Babylon who, according to the royal inscriptions, had 'grown up like a young puppy' at the Assyrian court.

Yet the challenge of navigating anti- and pro-Assyrian politics in Babylonia proved too difficult and Bel-ibni, accused of conspiring with the former, was replaced in 700 BC by Sennacherib's son Assur-nadin-shumi. An image of the new king of Babylon is carved on a so-called *kudurru* (boundary stone) or *naru* (standing stone), a long-established object in Babylonia used to record royal grants to high-ranking individuals of land, tax exemptions and privileges. It is evident from this small monument (some 16 centimetres/6 in. high) that Assur-nadin-shumi presented himself as a traditional Babylonian ruler. He wears the crown of Babylon and is named in the cuneiform inscription that covers the back and front of the monument. Above the king is a so-called *mushhushu* snake-dragon, the sacred animal of several important deities, including Marduk, the supreme god of Babylon.

While Assur-nadin-shumi was being installed, an Assyrian army had marched into the Babylonian marshes to crush a rebellion by another powerful local tribal leader, Mushezib-Marduk of Bit-Dakkuri, who had gathered his forces in opposition. Having successfully forced Mushezib-Marduk to flee, the Assyrian army next advanced into the territory of Marduk-aplu-iddina, who retreated with his followers to Elam.

By 694 BC intelligence reports probably indicated to Sennacherib that the exiled Babylonians were ready to make a new bid for the country. A plan was devised whereby the Assyrians would attack the enemy camp in Elam with a naval expedition across the head of the Persian Gulf. Boats of Phoenician design were built by Syrian specialists, brought down the Tigris and dragged to a canal

Monument showing Assur-nadin-shumi as king of Babylon, *c.* 700 BC.

connected to the Euphrates. Soldiers, horses and equipment were loaded aboard and floated down the river while the rest of the Assyrian army, led by the king, marched along the bank. At the Persian Gulf they waited for the sea to calm before the expedition set sail and, once ashore, engaged the Babylonians in battle.

The plan appeared to be working, but northern Babylonia had been left vulnerable with Sennacherib's forces engaged on the coast. The Elamite king, Hullushu-Inshushinak, therefore moved his army onto the plains around Sippar, capturing the city and receiving Assur-nadin-shumi, who was betrayed to him by some Babylonian nobles. Sennacherib's son was taken captive to Elam and Hallushu-Inshushinak's forces successfully fought off an attack by Assyrian troops while the Elamite king installed his own representative on the throne of Babylon.

Sennacherib's forces counterattacked and a fierce struggle continued into the following year. While the Assyrian army was able to claim much Babylonian territory, it was unable to regain control of the northwest of the country, including the city of Babylon, where Mushezib-Marduk now took the throne. It must have been very obvious that he would have to confront Sennacherib's forces if he had any hope of maintaining his position and so in 692 BC the new Babylonian king took gold and silver from the treasury of Marduk's temple and, according to the Assyrian royal inscriptions, sent it to the Elamite king saying, 'Gather your army, muster your forces, hurry to Babylon, and align yourself with us! Let us put our trust in you.'[76] The offer was accepted and a vast army was formed that included soldiers from across Babylonia, Elam and various small kingdoms of southwest Iran. The very next year the mercenary forces marched into the region close to Sippar, where they engaged an Assyrian army in a bloody battle. Although the result of the conflict appears to have been indecisive it was described using poetic language by the royal scribes at Nineveh, glorifying Sennacherib as the ultimate victorious warrior:

> I [Sennacherib] raged up like a lion, then put on armour and placed a helmet suitable for combat on my head. In my anger, I rode quickly in my exalted battle chariot, which lays enemies

> low. I took in my hand the mighty bow that the god Assur had granted to me and I grasped in my hand an arrow that cuts off life.
>
> I roared loudly like a storm and thundered like the god Adad against all of the troops of the wicked enemies. By the command of the god Assur, the great lord, my lord, I blew like the onset of a severe storm against the enemy on their flanks and front lines. With the weapons of the god Assur, my lord, and my fierce battle array, I turned them back and made them retreat. I slit their throats like sheep and thus cut off their precious lives like thread.[77]

In 690 BC the city of Babylon came under siege by the Assyrian army. For fifteen months the inhabitants suffered increasingly terrible conditions of famine and starvation as Mushezib-Marduk's allies gradually abandoned him or were defeated. In 689 BC his chief ally, the Elamite king, suffered a serious stroke and in the same year Babylon fell. Sennacherib now took revenge on the rebellious population that had cost him his son:

> I blew in like the onset of a tempest . . . I destroyed, devastated, and burned with fire the city and its buildings, from the foundations to its crenellations. I tore out brick and earth, as much as there was, from the inner and outer city wall, the temples, and the ziggurat, and threw them into the Arahtu river. I dug canals into the centre of that city and levelled the site with water. I destroyed the outline of its foundations to make its destruction even greater than that by the Flood, so that in future the site of that city and temples would be unrecognizable. I dissolved it in water and reduced it to meadowland.[78]

This is certainly more poetic licence by the Assyrian scribes as the city continued to exist, albeit badly scarred and impoverished. The symbols of the city's wealth and cultural prestige, the palaces and temples, were looted and ruined. The great religious cults, especially that of the god Marduk, were suspended, which resulted in huge psychological and economic loss for the city. It would be many years before Babylon's fortunes would be revived under Sennacherib's successor, Esarhaddon. Rebellion against Assyria had come at great cost.

Mass resettlement

> The town of Hesa, a road station of mine, lacks people; the postmaster and the commander of the recruits are there alone and cannot attend to it properly. Now, let me [Sargon II's provincial governor Bel-liqbi] get together 30 families and place them there. There are men of Nabu-salla the prefect living in Hesa, a cohort of craftsmen; let him move them out, settle them in the town of Argite, and give them fields and gardens.[79]

Against a backdrop of date palms, heavy with fruit, a number of people are on the move. A woman sits on a mule with a young boy who holds tightly to his mother while turning back to look at those following. A man with quiver and spears walks ahead of two women, one carrying a baby in her arms, the other laden with a sack and bag. At the far right a soldier holds the severed head of an enemy in each hand.

Babylonian deportees on the move following an Assyrian campaign, Nineveh, *c.* 690 BC.

The scene is part of a sequence of relief panels that lined the walls of a small room in the Southwest Palace at Nineveh and depicts the aftermath of an Assyrian campaign in southern Babylonia around 700 BC. The imagery continued across another stone panel – as recorded in a drawing made at the time of its excavation – revealing that the people were moving towards the Assyrian king, who is named in an accompanying cuneiform inscription: 'Sennacherib, king of the universe, king of Assyria, booty from the marshes of Sahrina passed before me.'[80]

A parade of booty, including human captives, following a successful military campaign is far from unusual. As early as the third millennium BC, Mesopotamian royal art and texts describe the raw materials, manufactured objects and large numbers of people captured by kings through violence and pillage. Enemy soldiers might be mutilated, executed or, if they were lucky, integrated into the victorious army, while other people could be put to work, perhaps as slaves. Yet this is not what we see depicted in the Assyrian reliefs. Perhaps instead it can be understood as a depiction of displaced populations, some of whom may have fled in advance of the Assyrian attack, but others were forced to move as their settlements were occupied and sacked. It might seem appropriate, therefore, to compare the scene with modern photographs and films of refugees fleeing for their lives. But again, that would be to misunderstand the message of the carving. The men, women and children passing before Sennacherib represent a well-practised Assyrian policy of deporting people, very often entire families, from conquered territory and their resettlement in other parts of the empire.

Deportation certainly played a part in the dismantling of enemy groups but its most important role was the provision of a workforce, especially for the Assyrian heartland, which became increasingly densely populated with hundreds of villages and towns. The aim was to fill holes in agricultural production and support major building projects, including, of course, the creation in turn of Kalhu, Dur-Sharrukin and Nineveh, as well as large-scale irrigation projects. With the expansion of the Assyrian state during the second half of the eighth century BC there was a doubling of the area under direct administrative control and a demand in many areas for additional human workers. All provinces were expected to provide a similar level of economic output and taxation, regardless of their size and population, and so one of the most important tasks of any provincial governor and their officials was to make this a reality by transferring people from one region to another in order to ensure agricultural production, as well as to complete infrastructure projects such as canal building or to populate new urban centres to stimulate economic growth. The result was that, over more than a century, hundreds of thousands, if not millions, of people were moved around a large area of the Middle East in a coordinated way with the aim of achieving a level of political, economic and cultural uniformity and stability across the empire. This was clearly a remarkable administrative feat, one that came at a cost for some but to the benefit of others.

Workers were an important resource and a degree of care was taken to ensure that deportees arrived at their destination safely and in good physical condition. The carved images of them on the palace walls show people travelling on animals and carts in family groups. It is clear from administrative documents, such as the letter quoted below, that they could be supplied with provisions such as food and clothing for the journey:

> As for the Aramaeans about whom the king my lord has written to me: 'Prepare them for their journey!' I shall give them their food supplies, clothes, a waterskin, a pair of shoes and oil. I do not have my donkeys yet, but once they are available, I will dispatch my convoy.[81]

The palace reliefs are consistent in showing deportees as moving in ordered lines without any indication of their mistreatment. Indeed, the intended message of such scenes, and one that is mirrored in the royal inscriptions, is that deportation is a positive thing, presented as an opportunity for a better future. This attitude is recorded in the Hebrew Bible, through a speech made by Sennacherib's representatives to the people of Jerusalem as the Assyrian army was laying siege to the cities of Judah in 701 BC. After urging them not to support Hezakiah, the Assyrian king promised,

> Make your peace with me and come out to me! Then every one of you will eat of his own vine, and every one of you will eat of his own fig tree, and every one of you will drink the water of his own cistern, until I come and take you away to a land like your own land, a land of grain and wine, a land of bread and vineyards, a land of olive trees and honey, that you may live, and not die! (2 Kings 18:31–2)

For some, perhaps many, this may have been a tempting offer – the families on the move from Lachish (see page 125) may have been relieved to be leaving their ruined city with such an offer. Once people had been moved and resettled at the state's expense they acquired the same legal rights and obligations as Assyria's other subjects; the primary requirement for becoming Assyrian was to pay taxes. Meanwhile, the most valued deportees – the elite families, specialist craftsmen and expert scholars – were rehoused and put to work in the cities of the Assyrian heartland.

It is certain, however, that for large numbers of people the process of deportation would have been difficult and even dangerous. The journey itself could be gruelling, travelling for many hundreds of kilometres with meagre rations, and individuals, especially women and children, were left open to abuse. It was not unusual for some war captives to be distributed among Assyrian troops and sold into slavery. Nor should we lose sight of the impact that this would have had on individual and group identity as families and communities were broken up, potentially leaving people behind in depopulated regions where the absence of workers would have had a negative impact on the local economy.

Scenes showing deportees, such as the one that introduced this section, were among the principal themes of Sennacherib's palace reliefs. These images, together with his inscriptions, suggest that he had more people moved across the empire than any of his predecessors or successors and reflect the movement of populations on a truly industrial scale. It has been calculated that perhaps close to half a million people, almost half of whom came from Babylonia, were moved and resettled during his reign.[82] Most deportees were destined for Nineveh, where, as we will see, they were set to work on a massive programme of construction, including city walls, palaces, temples and an extensive network of water reservoirs, canals and aqueducts.

Transforming the world

> After I [Esarhaddon] built and completed that palace from its foundations to its parapets and filled it with splendour, its mortar was mixed with fine beer, its clay was mixed with wine . . . I finished its work with rejoicing, jubilation, and melodious songs, and I named it 'The palace that administers everything.'[83]

Palatial residences were established across the empire as well as in the heartland for members of the royal family. It was, however, the creation or refurbishment of entire cities and the reshaping of the surrounding landscape that were the ultimate expressions of the king's power; only he had the authority and resources to remodel the physical world, which he achieved through the support and blessing of his gods.

In moving his court to Nineveh, Sennacherib initiated a massive building project for its enlargement. The city was enclosed by a 12-kilometre (7½ mi.) fortified double wall with moats. Called the 'Wall Whose Brilliance Overwhelms Enemies', this great structure enclosed an area nearly four times that of the existing city. It was punctuated by fifteen monumental gates that were individually named – for example, the Mashki Gate, meaning 'Gate of the Watering Places'; Nergal Gate, which may have served a ceremonial purpose, being the only one flanked by monumental human-headed winged bulls; Adad Gate; Ishtar Gate; Harbour Gate; and Halzi Gate. Within the city, the focus of work was on the summit of two ancient settlement mounds or tells, which were cleared of some buildings and stabilized. On top of the Kouyunjik mound was constructed the great Southwest Palace that the king named 'Palace Without a Rival', while on the smaller Nebi Yunus mound an arsenal for the storage of equipment and the marshalling of troops was erected.[84] These monumental structures loomed over the city, which was laid out below. Let us here turn to Sennacherib's own description of what was accomplished:

> Since time immemorial earlier kings, my ancestors . . . had not shown interest in the palace inside Nineveh, the seat of lordly dwelling whose site had become too small; nor had anyone conceived of and put his mind towards the straightening of the city's streets and the widening of its squares, the dredging of the river, and the planting of orchards . . . the performing of this work came to my attention by the will of the gods and I put my mind to it. I forcibly removed the people of southern Babylonia, Aramaean tribes, the land of the Manneans, and the lands Que and Hilakku, who had not submitted to my yoke, then I made them carry baskets of earth and they made bricks.
>
> I had a palace of elephant ivory, ebony, boxwood, *musukkannu*-wood, cedar, cypress, juniper, and terebinth, a palace that I named 'The Palace Without a Rival', constructed as my royal residence.
>
> I planted alongside it a botanical garden, a replica of Mount Amanus, which has all kinds of aromatic plants and fruit trees, trees that are the mainstay of the mountains and Babylonia, collected inside it.
>
> To plant gardens, I subdivided the meadowland upstream of the city into plots . . . for the citizens of Nineveh and I handed them over to them. To make those planted areas luxuriant, I cut with iron picks a canal straight through mountain and valley, from the border of the city Kisiri to the plain of Nineveh. I caused an inexhaustible supply of water to flow for a distance of one and a half leagues from the Khosr River and made it gush through feeder canals into those gardens.[85]

The supply of water to the growing city was essential for people and animals, and to expand the productivity of the surrounding agricultural land by irrigating farmland. The building of canals had long been a feature of Assyrian royal activity, but now Sennacherib initiated projects on a remarkable scale by making full use of the

Drawing of Sennacherib's cliff reliefs at Khinis (Bavian), *c.* 690 BC, from John Henry Wright, *A History of All Nations*, vol. II (1905), p. 92.

deportees brought into the heartland.[86] Taking advantage of the natural terrain, he redirected the water that flowed in streams, wadis and rivers to the Tigris from the steep foothills of the Zagros Mountains that enclose Assyria to the north and east. This relied on grand and complex hydraulic engineering systems. Their focus was the river Khosr, which ran through the middle of Nineveh. Strong river walls were built to contain it and then water was diverted to it in a series of massive canals, some of which were 100 metres (328 ft) wide and up to 20 metres (65 ft) deep. Some of the water brought in this way travelled nearly 60 kilometres (37 mi.). Along its course it passed over stone-built aqueducts; an example at the site of Jerwan was 280 metres (920 ft) long and 22 metres (72 ft) wide, and is estimated to have been constructed with half a million cut-stone blocks, many of which had cuneiform inscriptions naming Sennacherib, with five corbelled arches that spanned a valley.[87]

At the site of Khinis, some 50 kilometres (30 mi.) to the north of Nineveh, a series of monumental reliefs were carved in the cliff face overlooking the start of the canal system. They show Sennacherib in the presence of his gods, a theme also found in reliefs that lined stretches of the canals along their routes. These images were intended to stress the divine support of a powerful monarch who was capable of redirecting rivers, populating Assyria (albeit forcibly) and bringing abundance through new farmland and parks, including recreating the landscapes of conquered territories. The canals not only served to bring water for people, animals and plants, but enabled the movement of bulky agricultural produce and building materials (including the huge slabs of stone for lining the palace walls and gateways with reliefs and *lamassus*).

The king's scholars

> The king, my lord, keeps on saying to me [Urad-Nanaya, Esarhaddon's Chief Physician]: 'Why do you not diagnose the nature of this illness of mine and bring about its cure?' . . . Let the king apply this lotion and perhaps this fever will leave the king, my lord.[88]

The appointment of loyal and experienced administrators and soldiers to positions of authority at court and across the empire was, of course, crucial for good governance. The king, however, also relied on a range of scholars and skilled craftsmen who were masters of a vast field of knowledge extending across religion and science.[89] Although this wisdom was believed to have been given to humans by the gods in a distant mythological time, it needed to be continuously updated based on the latest thinking and, as the scholars depended on royal patronage, this created a highly competitive atmosphere as they vied for the king's attention.[90]

There were five main scholarly professions whose skills were available to those who could afford them: the *ashipu*, or exorcist; the *asu*, or physician; the *kalu*, or lamentation priest; the *tupsharru Enuma Anu Enlil*, or astrologer; and the *baru*, or diviner.

Ashipus were specialists – usually men, though there are occasional references in the texts to women – who spent years mastering magical–medical knowledge and treatments. In Assyria illness was understood as having supernatural origins, usually the result of an attack by a demon or the ghost of either somebody who had been known to the patient or a complete stranger. A person would become a target as a result of a transgression, perhaps inadvertently, against the gods or their ancestors (such as not providing the necessary offerings of food and drink for the dead). The *ashipu*'s job was to look for ominous signs on and around the patient to help identify the reasons for a god's displeasure and then, using medicines and magical rituals, convince them to remove the illness by driving out the offending ghost or demon.

A great deal is known about one family of exorcists in Ashur thanks to the survival of texts written by the chief *ashipu*, Kisir-Assur, and his apprentices in the time of kings Assurbanipal and Assur-etel-ilani.[91] As a trainee, with the help of his father, Kisir-Ashur gained a knowledge of magic spells and rituals alongside an understanding of areas that today we might classify under anatomy, paediatrics and veterinary medicine. In addition, he also learnt practical skills such as techniques of bandaging and of mixing and administering emetics. In one instruction manual, written in 658 BC, Kisir-Assur describes how to treat a patient suffering from ghost-induced confusion: he should sweep the ground, sprinkling it with purified water; set up an incense burner and pour a libation of beer; make a figurine of the ghost from clay, tallow and wax; the patient should then hold the figurine up to the god Shamash while reciting an incantation.[92]

A close associate of the *ashipu* was the *asu*. Although often described today as a physician, the *asu*'s specialism was to help a patient by reducing their discomfort through therapeutic means, such as applying medications made from plants, minerals and animal products. Here, for example, is the record of a symptom and 'cure' applied by an *asu*:

> If a man's head burns with fever and the hair of his head falls out and he repeatedly suffers pulsating arteries in the temples – to cure him shave his head, pound one shekel of bat guano in oil, cool down his head and bind it on; do not untie it for three days.[93]

Further reassurance for the patient was no doubt also provided by the *kalu*, whose job was to soothe and placate the anger of the gods through chanting.

When a king fell ill he could rely on the most experienced specialist to treat him, although, as is clear from the excerpt of a letter to Esarhaddon from his chief physician Urad-Nanaya that begins this section, at times diagnosis could be challenging. It seems that Esarhaddon in particular was constantly ill, often withdrawing to his quarters suffering from fever and dizziness, vomiting, diarrhoea and earaches. It might easily be concluded that the king was under supernatural attack.[94]

Along with lotions and spells, healers used amulets that were intended to help force evil beings to leave a sick person. Among the most terrifying supernatural forces they would engage with was a female demon called Lamashtu.[95] Whereas other demons and ghosts might cause illness largely as a result of human error or misfortune, Lamashtu appears to have been unique in that she was by her very nature evil and aggressive. Everybody was vulnerable to attack from Lamashtu, although it was her targeting of pregnant women and young children that was especially abhorrent. She is also unusual in being recognizable in Assyrian art, the intention no doubt to reveal and 'name and shame' her in order to allow her to be swiftly driven away. Lamashtu is shown as a monstrous composite, often with the head of a dog or a lion with ass's ears, a hairy or spotted body with naked breasts, long fingers and the talons of a bird; a piglet and a puppy suckle at her breasts and she holds snakes in her hands. She is represented in the lower register of the bronze amulet plaque shown here, riding a donkey in a boat that floats along a river that will carry her away along with the sickness she causes. Shown beside Lamashtu are objects that act as bribes intended to encourage her to leave: a comb, a mirror, a spindle and, a little more surprisingly to our eyes, the lower leg of a donkey.

One of the most effective ways of driving Lamashtu away, however, was to evoke her powerful adversary, the wind demon Pazuzu.[96] He is shown to the left of Lamashtu, striding with one arm raised to attack her. Pazuzu is also depicted in Assyrian art with standardized features: a canine-like grinning face with big eyes, a scaly body, a snake-headed penis, the talons of a bird, a scorpion's tail and wings. More dramatically, he appears on the back of this amulet with his head reaching over the edge, presumably to give reassurance to the sick person and to frighten Lamashtu. The patient himself is also shown on the plaque, lying on a bed accompanied by mythological figures; the fish-men are a type of *apkallu*, the ancient sages who are also represented on the wall reliefs of royal palaces. They can be understood as equivalent to the human *ashipu* and perhaps *asu* who magically remove Lamashtu by evoking the power of the great gods; these supreme deities appear on the plaque in symbolic forms in the top register above a row of protective spirits.

The last two types of scholar on our list were also learned specialists, but their role had less to do with healing and was more about understanding the will of the gods, especially when it came to the future. Assyrians understood the past, present and future to be part of a divine blueprint. This was not fixed and the fate of individuals could be changed through their own unintended actions or the work of evil agents. It was, however, possible to discover these past events and the future that would result from them through the skill of diviners who interpreted signs sent by the gods. Such divinely inspired omens were delivered as judgements, but through sacrifice, prayers and rituals, individuals could appeal to the gods to change their decisions, just as if they were in a law court or had sent a petition to the king as the source of justice. In this way, the effects of events that had happened in the past could be corrected to ensure that a negative future was turned into a positive one.

One type of diviner was the *tupsharru Enuma Anu Enlil*. They were extremely learned individuals who understood detailed omen lists, including a very large series of texts (some seventy tablets' worth) that derived from celestial events. The movement of the stars, planets and other phenomena in the sky were considered messages written by the gods, the meaning of which could be interpreted by consulting records of such occurrences in the past and what they suggested might happen as a result. All such omens were thought to affect the king and the state and so were of special interest to the royal court, where there was much competition between specialists to have their knowledge heard and supported. The observation of signs sent by the gods on earth was also important and there were many series of omens devoted to them. The longest one, called 'If a city', contains about 10,000 omens and covers everything from fire to the flight of birds and the appearance of animals and humans, as well as demons and other supernatural beings.[97]

Last, but far from least, was the *baru*. They posed questions to the gods Shamash and Adad while sacrificing an animal, especially a sheep – we see the specialist in action on a relief from the throne room in the Northwest Palace at Kalhu. After whispering a question in the animal's ear and inviting the gods to write an answer into the body parts, the slaughtered animal was systematically examined for signs. The organs were considered the most informative, especially the colour and shape and markings on a liver. The question was posed with the wish 'Shamash, great lord, give me a firm positive answer to what I am asking you!'

Individual features of the organs were investigated separately and more positive results than negative ones meant an overall 'yes' and vice versa. The answer was always a straightforward 'yes' or 'no' (literally 'favourable' or 'unfavourable'). Failures to achieve a clear result would be explained as errors in the procedure and more animals would be slaughtered to both placate the god and to achieve a clear outcome. It was, however, only possible to repeat the procedure three times before it was necessary to wait to have another go. More than one expert might be tasked with the same question to test the results. Many reports survive of the questions asked of the gods, not least in the royal archives. Here, for example, the gods

Bronze Lamashtu plaque, without provenance, *c.* 700–600 BC.

Baru diviner examining the entrails of a sacrificed sheep, Kalhu, *c.* 870 BC.

are asked to indicate whether a diplomatic marriage between an Assyrian princess and a ruler of powerful eastern Iranian horse nomads would have a positive outcome: 'If Esarhaddon, King of Assyria, gives him a royal daughter in marriage, will Bartatua, king of the Scythians, speak with Esarhaddon, King of Assyria, in good faith, true and honest words of peace?'[98]

Incantations, magic circles, fumigation, animal sacrifice, the reading of omens and the making and destroying of figurines were among the specialist tools intended to avoid bad outcomes and dispel evil. When it came to supernatural threats against the king, however, special measures were needed and, if the omens were especially bad, the 'substitute king ritual' was evoked.[99] A man – probably a criminal or opponent – was chosen by the king's high officials and experts, and enthroned with the royal regalia; he was given a queen and held court. The real king, meanwhile, kept a low profile and, although he never relinquished power, might be addressed in official correspondence as 'farmer' so that the evil forces wouldn't recognize him. Meanwhile, soon after being installed, the substitute king would recite all the evil that was predicted to befall the actual monarch, thereby inviting it onto himself (and the substitute queen). Once the danger had passed the substitute and his 'wife' were put to death – or, as the reports record more tersely, they went 'to their fate' – and were given an appropriately royal funeral. The real king could then resume normal duties. Not all substitute kings were, however, insignificant individuals. In a letter sent to King Esarhaddon, an Assyrian official reports on the installation as a substitute king of a man called Damqi who was the son of the chief administrator of Babylon's temples:

> Damqi, the son of the prelate of Akkad [Babylonia], who had ruled Assyria, Babylonia and all the countries, died with his queen on the night of the [?] day as a substitute for the king, my lord, and for the sake of the life of Shamash-shumu-ukin. He went to his fate for their redemption. We prepared the burial chamber. He and his queen were decorated, treated, displayed, buried and wailed over.[100]

The master scholars that the king relied upon were, of course, experts in reading and writing as well as in their field of specialism. They therefore could also be described by the term *tupsharru*, 'scribe'. As we have seen, this was also a title shared with thousands of other Assyrian men and women who had received some schooling and were employed at all levels of society. Their patron god was Nabu, whose symbol (which appears among those at the top of the Lamashtu plaque) was a writing stylus. There had been a temple dedicated to him at Kalhu when the city was established as the royal capital in the ninth century BC, but it was Sargon II who elevated Nabu to a place among the greatest gods of the Assyrian Empire. This move has been attributed to the king's military successes of 714 BC when the Assyrian army plundered the northern state of Musasir and its main temple, which contained enormous wealth.[101] Sargon describes his great triumph in a 'letter' addressed to Assur in which he reserves special praise for Nabu (who is paired with his father Marduk, god of Babylon):

> At the exalted command of Nabu and Marduk, who took a course through the positions of the stars that was a good omen for the taking up of my weapons, and favourable signs which mean the gaining of power . . . At the invaluable consent of the hero Shamash, who caused the liver to be inscribed with reliable omens that he would walk at my side . . . I took the road to Musasir, a difficult path.[102]

His scholars had therefore observed the planetary omens and confirmed them by taking sacrificial omens. In this way the specialists had proved their worth and as a result their skills – and of course their patron god, who was ultimately responsible – were placed at the heart of Assyrian kingship.

While Assyrian rulers had always highlighted in their inscriptions the skills bestowed on them by the gods, they increasingly stressed their learning and innate wisdom. Here, for example, is Sennacherib describing how he alone had solved the technical challenges of creating large-scale architectural features and sculptures in metal to adorn his new palace at Nineveh:

> Since time immemorial, the kings, my ancestors, created copper statues, replicas of their own forms, to be erected in temples, and through their manufacture they had exhausted all of the craftsmen . . . But as for me, Sennacherib, the foremost of all rulers, expert in every type of work, regarding large columns of copper and striding lion colossi, which none of the kings of the past who came before me had cast: with the ingenious mind that the prince, the god Ea [god of wisdom], had granted to me and taking counsel with myself, I intensively pondered how to perform this work. Then, with my own ideas and knowledge, I created a cast work of copper and expertly carried out its artful execution.[103]

It was, however, the last great king of Assyria, Assurbanipal, who especially stressed an identification with Nabu as 'crown prince of the gods', and therefore Marduk's heir. In some of his palace reliefs, for example, Assurbanipal presents himself wearing the diadem

Assurbanipal holding a hunting spear with the pens of a scholar in his belt, Nineveh, *c.* 650 BC.

of a crown prince rather than the high Assyrian royal headdress, and while other rulers might have shown themselves with a dagger in their belt, he is shown with two styli, the writing tool of scribes.[104] In his inscriptions, Assurbanipal presents himself as a scholar, one of the great experts in the scribal arts, and this allows him not only to interpret omens but to understand ancient texts imagined as coming from a mythical time 'before the Flood':

> I learned the craft of the sage Adapa, the secret and hidden lore of all the scribal arts. I am able to recognize celestial and terrestrial omens and can discuss them in an assembly of scholars. I am capable of arguing with expert diviners about the series 'If the liver is a mirror image of the heavens'. I can resolve complex mathematical divisions and multiplications that do not have an easy solution. I have read cunningly written texts in obscure Sumerian and Akkadian that are difficult to interpret. I have carefully examined inscriptions on stone from before the Flood that are sealed, stopped up and confused.[105]

Examples of cuneiform tablets written by Assurbanipal survive and suggest that he was certainly overstating his abilities. Nevertheless, this emphasis on both knowledge as a reflection of the king's power and his close relationship with the gods resulted in the accumulation of thousands of scholarly texts in the royal palaces at Nineveh. Tablets were actively collected from temple libraries, especially the ancient and venerable cultic centres in Babylonia, as well as from those belonging to experts themselves. These were then systematically re-copied and edited. Some 30,000 tablets and fragments survive and are commonly referred to today as a royal library; indeed, many of the tablets bear a short sentence stating that they belong to the palace, a 'library stamp' of sorts. This may have been an attempt at the gathering of universal knowledge as it was understood by Assurbanipal and his scholars, with the result that more than half of the texts were devoted to divination and procedures to appease the gods.[106] The tablets ranged widely across Assyrian scholarship, however, and included religious, medical, magical and ritual texts. There were also mythological tales and epics, not least accounts of the great hero king Gilgamesh, whose encounters with gods and his search for the meaning of life were as much an intellectual journey as a physical one. These narratives were fused with historic events in some of the palace wall reliefs, creating, as we will see, some of the greatest works of art from antiquity.

Depicting the world

> I [Sennacherib] engraved on large limestone slabs
> images of the enemy settlements that I had conquered.
> I surrounded the palace rooms' lower courses with
> them and made them an object of wonder.[107]

The design and carving of the palace wall reliefs that feature throughout this book involved many specialists. The most important people responsible for the overall decorative schemes of the palaces were likely to have been the scribal scholars. As experts in magic, religion and the ideology of kingship, they would have been able to determine the correct form and location of the images so that the protective spirits and the cultic messages could be magically effective. Similarly, the scribes who composed and edited the royal inscriptions would have probably devised the narrative messages of the painted and carved images. It is very likely that the king's approval was sought for at least the most important aspects of the design, as suggested by an official's letter to Esarhaddon:

> We have now sent two royal images to the king. I myself sketched the royal image which is an outline. They fashioned the royal image which is in the round. The king should examine them, and whichever the king finds acceptable we will execute accordingly. Let the king pay attention to the hands, the chin, and the hair.[108]

The stone used for the sculptures, with a few limestone exceptions, is gypsum. Blocks were quarried from outcrops in the Assyrian countryside on both sides of the river Tigris. Some details of the quarrying of the stone can be learnt from a series of reliefs that lined the walls of a courtyard in Sennacherib's palace at Nineveh. The hard work was largely undertaken by prisoners of war. Metal picks were used to extract the stone and it was then cut into blocks with long iron saws. For larger sculptures, like the gateway figures, the shape was roughed out in the quarries to reduce weight. The slabs were then dragged using levers and rollers through the countryside to the city. When the quarries were on the other side of the river, the stone was loaded onto rafts and floated across; the heaviest pieces would have to wait for the spring floods. The slabs destined for panelling the walls averaged between 2 and 3 metres (6½–10 ft) high and 30 centimetres (12 in.) thick. Individual slabs can weigh several tons, with the blocks for the largest gateway figures at Nineveh weighing as much as 40 tons.

The design of the relief was drawn across one side of a stone panel. The gypsum, a very soft stone, was incised easily with a metal point. This may have been undertaken in workshops where the slabs were laid out in rows, which would have been especially useful where the designs crossed successive panels. Some of the heavy work of removing the background may have also been accomplished here, although it is possible that the majority of work was done once the slabs had been set into place against the walls. Indeed, there is generally consistency of design within rooms, and differences between them suggest the allocation of rooms to certain individual draftsmen and teams of sculptors.

The panels were arranged along the mud-brick walls of the palaces, sunk a few centimetres into the ground onto a bed of bitumen, which allowed fine adjustments to be made in positioning them alongside other slabs. Metal dowels and clamps held the panels together and they were probably bracketed to the wall. The major carving was undertaken with metal points, used to chip away large areas of the surface, and metal chisels for smoothing. It would have been hard work and the tools would have needed constant sharpening. Points were again used for the fine incised details and it is possible that abrasives such as sand were used for the final finish. The reliefs were then painted.

Assyria victorious

> Through the support of the deities Assur, Sin, Shamash, Marduk, Nabu, Ishtar of Nineveh, Ishtar of Arbela, Ninurta, Nusku, and Nergal, I [Assurbanipal] constantly marched through the lands and established mighty victories.[109]

Assurbanipal was the last great king of Assyria. In 669 BC, three years after the empire had sworn allegiance to him as crown prince, his father Esarhaddon died en route to reimpose Assyrian power in Egypt. As planned, Assurbanipal took the Assyrian throne, and the following year his brother Shamash-shumu-ukin was crowned at Babylon. All was well. The treaty had apparently done its job. Stability at the centre meant that by 667 BC Assurbanipal was ready to confront the challenge posed by the Kushite king Taharqa, who had

Prisoners haul on ropes attached to a stone *lamassu* being dragged from a quarry, Nineveh, *c.* 690 BC.

succeeded in reasserting his authority through Egypt, his forces having removed the Assyrian garrison in the capital, Memphis. The Assyrian scribes report that their royal master took this affront very personally: 'A fast messenger came to Nineveh and reported this to me. My heart became enraged about these deeds and my temper turned hot.'[110]

The army was assembled and set out for Egypt, some 1,800 kilometres (1,120 mi.) from Nineveh. It was a major logistical challenge and a heavy draw on resources but it was achieved as in the past through the remarkable administrative and communication systems that maintained the empire. The account of the campaign is told by the scribes of Nineveh through the voice of the king and presented as an effortless advance followed by victory in a major battle in the Nile Delta:

> I mustered my elite forces that Assur and the goddess Ishtar had placed in my hands. I quickly advanced to support and aid the kings and officials who were in Egypt, servants who belonged to me, and I marched as far as the city of Kar-Banite. Taharqa, the king of Egypt and Kush, heard about the advance of my expeditionary force inside the city of Memphis, and mustered his battle troops before me to wage armed battle and war. With the support of the gods Assur, Bel, and Nabu, the great gods, my lords who march at my side, I brought about the defeat of his troops in a widespread pitched battle. Taharqa heard about the defeat of his troops while inside the city of Memphis. The awe-inspiring radiance of Assur and the goddess Ishtar overwhelmed him and he went into a frenzy. The brilliance of my royal majesty, with which the gods of heaven and netherworld had endowed me, covered him; he abandoned the city of Memphis and, in order to save his life, he fled inside the city of Thebes. I seized Memphis and then made my troops enter and reside there.[111]

Assurbanipal appointed governors from among the local pro-Assyrian nobility, selecting a certain Necho of the city of Sais as the primary ruler.

In 664 BC, however, Taharqa died and was succeeded by Tantamani, who brought renewed energy to the Kushite throne. He launched an invasion of the Nile Delta, defeating the local rulers who had sided with Assyria. In response an army was despatched from Nineveh, drawing on forces and supplies organized by provincial governors and vassals as it marched towards Egypt. In the words of Assurbanipal,

> For a second time, I took the direct road to Egypt and Kush. Tantamani heard about the advance of my expeditionary force and that I had set foot on Egyptian territory, he abandoned the city of Memphis and, in order to save his own life, he fled inside the city of Thebes. The kings, governors, and officials whom I had stationed in Egypt came to meet me and kissed my feet.
>
> I took the road in pursuit of Tantamani and I marched as far as the city of Thebes, his fortified city. He saw the assault of my battle array and abandoned Thebes; he fled to the city of Kipkipi. With the support of the god Assur and the goddess Ishtar, I conquered Thebes in its entirety.
>
> Silver, gold, precious stones, as much property of his palace as there was, garments with multi-coloured trim, linen garments, large horses, people – male and female – two tall obelisks cast with shiny metal, whose weight was 2,500 talents and which stood at a temple gate, I ripped them from where they were erected and took them to Assyria. I carried off substantial booty, which was without number, from inside the city of Thebes.[112]

With Egypt apparently contained and the depleted Assyrian treasury to some extent refilled, Assurbanipal turned his attention towards southwest Iran and the kingdom of Elam. The region was divided by rival camps supporting different claimants to the throne. Such political division served Assyria as it helped to ensure that Elam was distracted from its traditional attempts to dominate both Babylonia and the east Tigris region. By the 650s, however, a certain Tepti-Humban-Inshushinak, or, as the Assyrian scribes found more manageable, Teumman, took the Elamite throne. He repeatedly sent threatening letters to Assurbanipal demanding the extradition of members of the royal line whom he had ousted and who had been provided with sanctuary at Nineveh. Again the Assyrian king is presented as taking this as a personal insult:

> On account of these insolent words that Teumman had spoken, I made an appeal to the sublime goddess Ishtar. I stood before her, knelt down at her feet, and made an appeal to her divinity, while my tears were flowing . . . The goddess Ishtar who resides in the city of Arbela entered and she had quivers hanging on the right and left. She was holding a bow at her side and she was unsheathing a sharp sword that was ready to do battle.[113]

The text then changes to the third person, as if recounted by a witness to the encounter between the goddess and king:

> The goddess Ishtar, the sublime of the gods, called out to you, instructing you, saying: 'You are looking forward to waging war and I myself am about to set out towards the battlefield'. You then said to her: 'Let me go with you, wherever you go, O Lady of Ladies!' She replied to you, saying: 'You will stay in the place where you are currently residing. Eat food, drink wine, make music, and revere my divinity. In the meantime, I will go and accomplish this task, thus I will let you achieve your heart's desire. Your face will not become pale, your feet will not tremble, you will not wipe off your sweat in the thick of battle'. She took you into her sweet embrace and protected your entire body. Fire flared up in front of her. She went off furiously outside. She directed her attention towards Teumman, the king of the land of Elam with whom she was angry.[114]

With divine blessing, Assurbanipal therefore remained at Nineveh while an Assyrian army marched south to confront the Elamite forces of Teumman. The encounter between the Assyrian and Elamite armies near Susa at the site of Til-Tuba beside the river Ulai was retold in a series of remarkable reliefs that lined the walls of a large chamber in the Southwest Palace at Nineveh. The sculptors made

The chaos of battle and the execution of Teumman at Til-Tuba, Nineveh, *c.* 650 BC.

use of undecorated slabs of beautiful limestone that Assurbanipal's grandfather Sennacherib had obtained from sources some 200 kilometres (125 mi.) to the north of the capital. These reliefs are among the greatest achievements of Assyrian art. Every part of the composition is packed with details of soldiers, animals and chariots to produce what appears at first sight to be a meaningless explosion of figures which, nevertheless, wonderfully expresses the chaos of war. Closer inspection, however, reveals a tightly controlled vision, with Assyrian soldiers forcing the enemy Elamites down a hill in an unstoppable movement across the panels to the right. In the centre of the scene several narratives are played out along a series of parallel ground lines: Teumman tumbles from his chariot and, fleeing to the right into a seemingly claustrophobic woodland, is caught and decapitated. In triumph, an Assyrian soldier carries the severed head left across the field. These chilling images are carefully captioned with incidental details and even speeches by the enemy. The registers of narrative dissolve on the far right and the Elamites tumble into a river which, along with the hill, acts to frame the entire composition. Teumman is easily identifiable in the narrative as his robes and crown distinguish him from the surrounding Elamite soldiers, but unusually his face is shown with distinct physical features: a cropped beard, shoulder-length hair, hooked nose, tightly closed left eye and, when his hat falls off at one point, a receding hairline. This is almost certainly not a portrait as we might think of one today, in other words a visual representation of what the man actually looked like. Instead this is closer to a caricature constructed from the physical features identified by Assyrian scholars as signs sent from the gods that revealed Teumman to be a weak and evil individual, a man not fit to rule.[115] His imagery is therefore in complete contrast with portraits of the Assyrian monarch, which always depict a perfect image of kingship.

The Til-Tuba battle reliefs decorated a wall on one side of a doorway, on the opposite side of which were reliefs depicting the aftermath of the battle with the Assyrians installing their appointee in Elam and the torture and humiliation of surviving rebel leaders. The arrangement of these scenes into strict registers with neat rows of Assyrian soldiers and prostrating Elamites represents the ordered world as restored by Assurnasirpal and contrasts with the perceived chaos of Teumman's rule.

The challenges of managing the complex politics of Elam were nothing, however, compared with those of Babylonia. Control of the southern country had always been a problem for the Assyrians and they had tried many approaches: Sennacherib had lost a son in his attempt, ruining the city of Babylon in punishment, while Esarhaddon sought to establish stability and order by investing huge sums in restoring the city to its former glory. Shamash-shamu-ukin, ruling from Babylon, faced significant pressures in navigating the

The severed head of Teumman transported to Nineveh, *c.* 650 BC.

pro- and anti-Assyrian groups and the intrigues of the leaders of wealthy tribes and ancient cities. He was drawn towards the anti-Assyrian camp which sought Babylonian independence. The royal inscriptions of Nineveh stress – as is typical for this date – that his decision was motivated by opposition, presumably in a fit of jealousy, to his bother in Assyria. There might have been some truth in this but it may be wrong to read too much into the complaints of Assurbanipal, as given voice by his scribes:

> As for Shamash-shumu-ukin, my unfaithful brother for whom I performed many acts of kindness and whom I had installed as king of Babylon . . . he forgot these acts of kindness that I had done for him and constantly sought out evil deeds. Aloud, with his lips, he was speaking friendship, but deep down, his heart was scheming for murder. He lied to the citizens of Babylon who had been devoted to Assyria, servants who belonged to me, and he spoke words of deceit with them. In a crafty manoeuvre, he sent them to Nineveh, before me, to inquire about my well-being.
>
> While those citizens of Babylon stayed in Assyria obediently awaiting my decisions, he, Shamash-shamu-ukin, my unfaithful brother who did not honour my treaty, incited the people of the land of Akkad, Chaldea, Aram, and the Sealand [different areas of Babylonia] servants who belonged to me, to rebel against me.[116]

In 652 BC Shamash-shumu-ukin 'locked the city gates of Sippar, Babylon, and Borsippa and then broke off our brotherly relations. On the walls of those cities, he posted his fighting men and they were constantly doing battle with me.'[117] The Assyrians rapidly forced Shamash-shumu-ukin to withdraw into Babylon but only in the second of two major battles were they able to inflict a serious defeat on the Babylonians. While Assurbanipal's scribes write of countless victories against the opposing forces, including those of the Elamites and Arabs, the war dragged on and descriptions of plague, famine and starvation across the country probably offer a more accurate reflection of reality. The resources of the empire, however, gradually gained the upper hand and by 650 BC Babylon was under siege, as were the cities of Borsippa, Cutha and Sippar. In the south, the pro-Assyrian city of Ur was under extreme pressure from Elamite and local Chaldean tribes. Eventually, Assyrian troops arrived and the city was rescued. After two years of the most terrible suffering by the inhabitants of Babylon, the city walls were breached and the great settlement was plundered and torched; Assurbanipal's brother died in the flames – an outcome understood by the Assyrian king as determined by the gods themselves: 'The deities Assur, Sin, Shamash, Adad, Bel, Nabu, Ishtar of Nineveh, Sharrat-Kidmuri, Ishtar of Arbela, Ninurta, Nergal, and Nusku, who march before me and kill my foes, consigned Shamash-shumu-ukin, my hostile brother who had started a fight against me, to a raging conflagration and destroyed his life.'[118]

Fighting may have continued in the south of Babylonia following the fall of the capital but by 646 BC the Assyrian army had advanced into Elam, where Susa and other major cities were sacked. Finally, Arab tribes of the western desert who had supported the Babylonians were attacked and some of their chiefs deposed.

Assurbanipal marked the successes of his army with huge celebrations. A building on the citadel mound at Nineveh was constructed (the North Palace) and the king's victories were depicted in impressive wall reliefs. One large chamber, often identified as the throne room, was decorated with scenes of the triumph in Elam placed opposite scenes of victories in Egypt, perhaps intended to evoke the extent of the empire from east to west. Assurbanipal is entirely absent from such battle scenes, which of course reflects the real situation. There is instead an interest in the suffering and humiliation of the enemy, where the king's main role is to receive defeated people and booty. Assurbanipal dominates such scenes, standing in his chariot, slightly magnified in scale and wearing his tall crown. Sometimes the image of the king occupies the entire height of a register with rows of smaller figures standing on lines before him, one above the other. One such image shows the presentation of the royal regalia from Babylon itself.

The finest sculptures from the North Palace are, without doubt, the scenes of Assurbanipal hunting and killing lions, the most powerful and dangerous animals in Assyria. As we have seen, the theme of the royal hunt was closely associated with the notion of Assyrian kingship and had been a popular motif in royal inscriptions and imagery from the second millennium BC onwards, most obviously in the image of the king grasping and stabbing a rampant lion that was carved on stamp seals used by the king's senior officials. However, Assurbanipal exploited the subject as never before in both literary texts and magnificent images. Reliefs depicting the king hunting lions decorated the corridors of the palace and reinforced the notion of a powerful king at the very heart of the empire. The carved slabs in one room had scenes of the king hunting lions from a chariot within an arena. These sporting scenes play with large areas of empty space to evoke the arena itself as well as the drama of the spectacle. We know from Assurbanipal's inscriptions that the hunting field was actually in Nineveh and was dedicated to the warrior goddess Ishtar. This is, therefore, a ritual act in which the killing of the eighteen lions may be a magical way of protecting the eighteen gates of the capital city.[119] The wild animals were brought to the arena in cages from the neighbouring plains. In reliefs elsewhere in the palace, lions and other animals are hunted

The royal regalia of Babylon presented to Assurbanipal, Nineveh, *c.* 645 BC.

Assurbanipal despatches a wounded lion, Nineveh, *c.* 645 BC.

in the wilderness: wild donkeys and gazelle that spoil pasture and farmland flee before the royal hunter. The use of a continuous narrative in which a lion is shown in multiple images rushing from his cage towards the king is a truly masterful use of a single space to explore the excitement of the confrontation. The most remarkable aspect of these superb reliefs is the way in which the sculptors have captured the naturalism of the animals as well as their terrible suffering. The aim of the artists was not to generate pity for the dying creatures but rather to highlight their raw, dangerous presence and to show how they collapse in agony at the hands of the Assyrian king who, through the support of the gods and the skill of his weapons, brings civilization to the chaotic and disordered world that the animals represent. Another scene shows Assurbanipal with the carcasses of lions at his feet pouring a liquid offering to the goddess Ishtar – it parallels an image in which he is shown pouring a libation over the severed head of Teumman.

The ultimate triumph of the king over the forces of chaos is depicted in a sculptural masterpiece that decorated a private room in the North Palace. It is a scene of Assurbanipal apparently relaxing with his queen Libbali-sharrat in a landscape of trees and vines. The royal couple are engaged in a banquet, celebrating with music the triumphs of Assyria over Elam as represented by the severed

head of Teumman hanging from the branches of a fir tree on the left of the panel. On the right of the scene, a long staff, held by a figure carved on the adjoining slab, scatters troublesome birds from a fir tree and a fruiting palm, the latter a tree associated with Babylonia and Elam whose people had similarly been scattered by the Assyrian army. Mirroring in stone the command of the goddess Ishtar given to Assurbanipal in advance of the battle of Til-Tuba – 'You will stay in the place where you are currently residing. Eat food, drink wine, make music, and revere my divinity' – the atmosphere is charged with symbolism and ritual import in which the king and the queen embody the gods in a lyrical image of beauty and power.[120]

Collapse

The great triumphs over Babylonia, Elam and Egypt, as well as against wild animals, as presented in the royal inscriptions and carved reliefs from Nineveh suggest that in the decade after 650 BC, Assyria had mastered the Middle East and Assurbanipal reigned

The 'Garden Party' with Assurbanipal and Libbali-sharrat, Nineveh, *c.* 645 BC.

supreme. Although the images evoke a vigorous and powerful monarch, this was perhaps in contrast with reality. There are good indications that all was not well. In the following years scholarly correspondence and official documentation peter out, major public building activity comes to a stop and royal inscriptions dry up – the last Assurbanipal inscription is written in Nineveh around 643 BC, while the latest one in Babylonia dates to 639 BC. What had happened?

Empire brought with it demands that could result in costs greater than the benefits. Military campaigns were hugely expensive and traditionally relied on plunder and tribute for their financing. By the time Assurbanipal had regained control of Babylonia from his brother and the Elamites, there may have been little left in either the Assyrian or the Babylonian treasuries. The impact of this took a few years to materialize but gradually pressure mounted, initially at the frontiers of the empire. In Egypt, Necho's successor Psamtek extended his control through the country and then looked to extend his authority over states bordering the eastern Mediterranean. Trouble was also emerging to the northeast of Assyria; as late as 643 BC the Urartian king Sarduri III had sent an embassy of friendship to Assurbanipal but in the following years sites across his kingdom were attacked and abandoned and Urartu disintegrated as Iranian Medes, who had come to dominate much of Armenia and western Iran, along with horse-riding Cimmerian tribes, captured territory.

In Assyria itself Assurbanipal appears to have made major changes to the way in which he governed; his most trusted advisers were no longer his military officers or his scholars but instead his domestic staff. Whether these changes were the result of an increasingly reclusive, out-of-touch monarch it is difficult to know, but they may well have generated resentment and dismay among senior officials. The king was at the heart of ritual and decision making and without good advisers there was much that could go wrong.

When Assurbanipal died around 630 BC he was succeeded by his son Assur-etil-ilani. The administrative documents that survive from his reign don't suggest any major problems. Babylonia also appeared secure under an Assyrian appointee called Kandalanu. When, however, both men died, probably in 627 BC in unknown circumstances, things started to unravel. Assur-etil-ilani was succeeded by Sin-shar-ishkun (626–612 BC), possibly a brother, but there were revolts in both Assyria and Babylonia. At Nineveh a general, Sin-shumu-lishir, attempted unsuccessfully to usurp the throne. Another general called Nabopolassar was, however, more successful in Babylonia. His forces repulsed an Assyrian army sent against him and, with the backing of some cities and tribal groups, who had a long list of grievances against Assyria, Nabopolassar was crowned in Babylon. Gradually the Babylonian king extended his authority across the country and by 616 BC he was launching attacks on Assyrian territory. Assyria resisted fiercely but after several months Nabopolassar had pushed north along the Euphrates into Syria. The following year the Babylonians attacked into Arrapha. The Assyrians managed to repulse them at Ashur but were then beaten at Takritain (modern Takrit) about 100 kilometres (60 mi.) to the south – the heartland of the empire was under significant threat.

The situation for Sin-shar-ishkun became even more dire when Umakishtar – better known today by the Latinized form of his name, Cyaxares – a powerful ruler of the Medes based at Ecbatana (modern Hamadan) in Iran, turned against him. The kings of Ecbatana had long benefited from close military and economic links with the Assyrian Empire, not least because the Medes controlled a major trade route linking the highlands of Iran with lowland Mesopotamia. Now Cyaxares recognized an opportunity as Assyrian forces were focused on confronting Nabopolassar, and in the summer of 614 BC he led his army through the Zagros Mountains into Assyria. The Medes besieged but failed to take Tarbisu, seat of the crown prince just to the north of Nineveh, but then turned on Ashur, which was captured. The ancient religious capital of Assyria was sacked; the tombs of the kings were looted, the sarcophagi smashed, the palaces and temples looted and torched. Probably around the same time Kalhu also fell and was ransacked.

Despite these catastrophes, Assyria's forces remained formidable and by the next year Sin-shar-ishkun led a counterattack into Babylonia. It was probably in these desperate times as armies attacked and counterattacked that a deal was struck between Nabopolassar and Cyaxares (later tradition claims that the alliance was sealed though the marriage of a daughter of Cyaxares with Nabopolassar's son Nebuchadnezzar). In 612 BC the combined Babylonian and Median armies, reinforced with contingents of steppe nomads (Cimmerians, Scythians, Bactrians), converged on Nineveh. The huge gates of the city were hastily narrowed as a defence against the coming assault but the very scale of the walls, some 12 kilometres (7½ mi.) with multiple entrances, meant it was always going to be difficult to secure its entire length. Nevertheless, the defences were sufficient for the city to hold out for some three months before the walls were breached and the city was stormed. A snapshot of the chaos and slaughter that followed is evident near the southeast corner of the city wall at the so-called Halzi Gate. Here, in the gate passageway, thirteen individuals died: a horse and rider and six men, three adolescents, three children and a baby, cut down by arrows.[121] The great palaces and temples of Nineveh were occupied and plundered. Was it at this point that Assurbanipal's library was ransacked or had Assyrian courtiers already gathered together many of these crucial documents to 'shred' them by smashing the tablets and ripping apart the scrolls and writing boards in order to prevent the information they contained falling into the hands of the enemy? We don't know. It is also unknown what happened to Sin-shar-ishkun, but he was almost certainly among those killed as the great city was overwhelmed.

In the days that followed the conquerors took revenge on both the inhabitants of the royal palaces and the symbols of their former power. At Kalhu, for example, more than one hundred prisoners were executed and thrown into one of palace wells; many had their hands and feet shackled and may have been hurled into the well while alive. The palace wall reliefs at both Kalhu and Nineveh were also the focus for another form of execution. Given that the images were understood as embodying a living essence of the individuals represented, figures of the king, queen and some officials were carefully identified and then mutilated, their faces chipped away and their wrists cut.[122] In one of Assurbanipal's lion-hunting reliefs,

A lion is magically released from the grasp of Assurbanipal by the severing of its tail, Nineveh, *c.* 645 BC.

the king is shown grabbing a lion's tail and preparing to strike the animal with a mace, but the tail has received repeated blows from a metal point, thereby magically freeing the lion from the king's grasp. Tablets containing the loyalty oaths sworn to Assurbanipal by some of the Medes were returned to Kalhu and deliberately smashed in the temple of Nabu, releasing the owners from their obligations to Assyria.[123] The enormous palaces and temples were then torched and abandoned.

Assyria was not quite beaten, however. A court gathered around Assur-uballit II at Harran (close to the modern border with Syria in southeastern Turkey). He could only be recognized as crown prince, however, since the loss of Ashur meant it was impossible for him to be crowned in the Assur temple and instead the ritual took place in Harran's temple of the moon god Sin; despite his choice of throne name, invoking the fourteenth-century ruler who had launched Assyria on the path to empire, his authority would probably have been greatly diminished by the lack of blessing by the supreme deity.[124]

In 611 BC Nabopolassar led his troops northwards, breaking apart the Assyrian administrative system by attacking such places as Tushhan (modern Ziyaret Tepe in Turkey), a provincial centre on the northern border of the former empire.[125] A letter written by an official called Mannu-ki-libbali describes the hopeless position of Tushhan in the face of the advancing enemy:

> Concerning the horses, Assyrian and Aramaean scribes, cohort commanders, officials, coppersmiths, blacksmiths, those who clean the tools and equipment, carpenters, bow-makers, arrow-makers, weavers, tailors and repairers, to whom should I turn? . . . Not one of them is there. How can I command? . . . The lists are not at my disposal. According to what can they collect them? Death will come out of it. No one [will escape]. I am done.[126]

It is possible that Assur-uballit appealed to Egypt for aid since he was joined at Harran by an Egyptian army. This may have been as much an attempt by Egypt to extend its own claims over the region as a desire to defend Assyria. In 610 BC Nabopolassar advanced on Harran, the Assyrian and Egyptian garrison withdrew and the city capitulated to the Babylonians. The following year Assur-uballit's soldiers and the Egyptian forces returned to lay siege to the city but were again forced to retreat. The last Assyrian ruler disappears from the records as any hope of a restoration was lost with Nebuchadnezzar's victory in battle against the Egyptians at Carchemish in 605 BC.

FIVE

The Aftermath of Empire

The bureaucratic systems that had held the empire together continued in some areas, where administrators simply dated their documents with the name of Cyaxares or Nabopolassar depending where they were writing.[1] In central Assyria, however, cuneiform writing ceased to be used as large parts of the population were deported to Babylonia or, as prisoners of war, were distributed as workers and slaves to elite soldiers of the conquering armies. Some groups may have fled to their historic homelands from where they or their ancestors had been deported by the Assyrians. Others simply sought security and employment elsewhere. As a result, the Assyrian country underwent a massive depopulation, and settlements shrank or were abandoned. Only scattered communities were left to maintain the cities as well as the extensive irrigation systems that had supported the previous populations with fresh water. Without upkeep, the canals and aqueducts soon became dilapidated, never to be used again, and the agricultural lands that also depended on them ceased to be farmed.

In Babylonia, despite the appalling damage and loss of life that had resulted from decades of conflict, the wealth and workforce that arrived as a result of victory meant a revival of the country's economy with investment in agriculture and buildings: under Nabopolassar's son and successor Nebuchadnezzar II (604–562 BC) the city of Babylon was transformed into a glorious replacement for Nineveh. The king ruled an empire almost as extensive as that of Assyria and he devoted much time and expense enforcing his authority over the previous provinces and vassals in Syria and the

Levant, while maintaining a careful watch on the surrounding mountains that were dominated by the Medes.

Although Assyria was without a king, capital and empire, Assyrian identity wasn't lost. Among the exiles at Uruk in southern Babylonia a small shrine was devoted to the god Assur, an idea that would have been unthinkable earlier when his only home was Ashur. Circumstances had dramatically changed. But the exiled deity would nevertheless return home following the conquest of Babylon by Cyrus the Great in 539 BC. He was king of the city of Anshan, an ancient centre of the Elamites, Babylonia's historic rival, but a region now populated by Iranian Persian tribes. Cyrus rapidly took control of the Median highlands and turned his attention to the lowlands of Babylonia, which fell before his army. With the capture of Babylon, the Persian king granted the restoration of cults uprooted from their homes by earlier rulers – so exiles from Judah set out to restore the worship of YHWH in Jerusalem, while, according to the so-called Cyrus Cylinder, the temple of Assur was re-established at Ashur:

> From Babylon I sent back to their places, to the sanctuaries across the river Tigris whose shrines had earlier become dilapidated, the gods who lived therein: to Ashur, Susa, Akkad, Eshnunna, Zamban, Meturan, Der, as far as the border of Gutium [the Zagros mountains]. I made permanent sanctuaries for them. I collected together all of their people and returned them to their settlements.[2]

The communities that arrived to restore the ruined city of Ashur were very much aware of its long and illustrious past, for into the restored temple to Assur were moved a large number of historic stone and clay texts relating to the deity and Assyrian kings dating from the early second millennium BC to the time of Sin-sharru-ishkun.[3] These inscribed objects had been gathered from across the city's temples, palaces and walls to memorialize Assyria's former glory and perhaps stand as an expectation of its revival.

The names of some of Assyria's most powerful kings were also preserved in popular stories circulating across the Middle East in

Aramaic, which would remain the common language of the region for another millennium. One of the earliest surviving examples is preserved on a fifth-century BC Aramaic papyrus from Egypt that tells a version of a story involving a man called Ahiqar – who may be inspired by an actual official of Esarhaddon.[4] Versions of the tale are known widely from later manuscripts written in Syriac, Armenian, Turkish, Georgian, Slavonic, Russian, Rumanian and Serbian, as well as Arabic. The hero is also known from the Book of Tobit in the Bible, as well as from Aesop's fables. The basic form of the story is this:

> Ahiqar was a councillor of King Sennacherib but, although both rich and powerful, he was a disappointed man owing to the fact he had been unable to father a son. But he was very clever and so, in order to pass on his learning and influence, he adopted his nephew Nadan. It soon became clear, however, that the young man was both ungrateful and unworthy, finally turning against Ahiqar by making a false accusation against him to the king. Sennacherib was enraged by what he had been told and decided to have his councillor executed. He sent for Nebosumiskun who was ordered to kill Ahiqar. It transpires, however, that in the past Ahiqar had saved Nebosumiskun from execution and so the grateful man hid the councillor and killed a slave instead. Since the wise Ahiqar was thought to be dead, the Egyptian Pharaoh took the opportunity to test the Assyrian king by asking him to send a man to perform an apparently impossible task in return for three years' worth of tribute from Egypt. If he failed the Assyrian king would have to pay his rival the same amount. In despair, the king mourned the death of Ahiqar, and so Nebosumiskun brought Ahiqar back to court. The king was delighted and sent Ahiqar to Egypt to carry out the Pharaoh's task. Ahiqar was successful and the Pharaoh lost his claim for tribute. When Ahiqar returned to Assyria he confronted and lectured Nadan who swelled up and died.

Another Aramaic papyrus from Egypt tells a story of the confrontation between King Sarbanabal (Assurbanipal) and his brother, Sarmuge (Shamash-shumu-ukin). It can be summarized thus:

> Sarbanabal sends Sarmuge to Babylonia as governor where his only responsibility, aside from feasting, is to ensure that the king receives his annual tribute. All is going well until on one occasion Sarmuge's emissaries arrive in Nineveh and, instead of tribute, they deliver an insulting letter. On the advice of his general, Sarbanabal ignores the insult and treats the visitors with great respect. Sarbanabal then summons his sister Saritrah and sends her to reason with Sarmuge. Saritrah travels to Babylon where she is challenged by the sentries at the palace gate and then rebuffed by her brother. She protests that she is not stubble to be trampled underfoot. Then Saritrah appeals to Sarmuge to return to Nineveh where, she tells him, he will be welcomed. In response, Sarmuge offers hospitality to Saritrah's horse! Annoyed, Saritrah blames the quarrel between the two brothers on Sarmuge who curses his sister. She prepares to leave and advises her brother to build a chamber, throw in pitch and incense, and then bring in his sons and daughters and physicians who – as his advisors – had made him an arrogant man. When the consequences of Sarmuge's actions become apparent, she tells him, he should set the place on fire and perish in the flames. With that Saritrah returns to Nineveh and reports her conversation to Sarbanabal who immediately orders an army be sent to Babylon to bring Sarmuge back alive. Faced by the Assyrian army and the threat of Babylon falling in three days, Sarmuge appears to agree to return to Nineveh. But instead of leaving immediately, he builds a chamber, throws in pitch and incense and brings in his children and advisors together.[5]

The end of the papyrus is very fragmentary but it seems that in this version of the story, Sarmuge actually sets out for Nineveh but dies on the way.

These popular reimaginings of Assyria's past glory permeated the lands that had formed the empire and were no doubt also preserved within Assyria itself, which was named in the Persian records as the province of Athuria and was gradually being repopulated. Villages and towns revived further following the conquest of the Achaemenid Empire by Alexander the Great between 336 and 323 BC, after which Assyria became part of the Hellenistic Seleucid Empire. A prosperous but relatively quiet backwater began to be transformed when the city of Hatra, lying some 50 kilometres (30 mi.) to the west of Ashur, was developed as a major centre under the Arsacid Parthian dynasty that from around 150 BC came to replace the Seleucids as the dominant power in Mesopotamia and Iran.[6] In the following centuries, as Hatra emerged as the centre of a wealthy Arab kingdom dominating the overland trade routes, Ashur benefited economically. This prosperity was reflected in the erection of a monumental temple over the earlier temple of Assur. Although it was laid out with Parthian-style long halls (*iwans*), the new temple followed the alignment and orientation of the older building. Monuments were now dedicated to Assur with inscriptions in Aramaic. The text on the inscribed stela shown here states it was erected in the 324th year of the Seleucid calendar, which is equivalent to the year AD 12 or 13. It is dedicated to the goddess Sherua (an alternative to Mullissu) and resembles the free-standing stela erected by Assyrian kings under the empire, suggesting an ongoing sense of continuity with the city's past.

Further north, Nineveh and Arbela were also flourishing within a kingdom called Adiabene. This region, however, became a battleground throughout the second and early third centuries AD, as the Parthians confronted Roman armies pushing east. Nevertheless, it was not Roman legions who defeated the Parthians. Instead they were overthrown in 224 by the Persians under the Sasanian king Ardashir. Hatra resisted but was captured and destroyed by the Sasanians around 240, while at Ashur the great temple of Assur was obliterated and the ancient city slid into terminal decline.

By this date Christianity had established itself as a significant religion across northern Mesopotamia. The Sasanians, who followed Zoroastrianism, were wary of a faith that became the official religion of Rome (in 380), and there were periods when Christians were persecuted. In the middle of the fifth century, however,

Stela dedicated to the goddess Sherua, Ashur, *c.* AD 12.

disagreements within the wider Christian community over the divine nature of Christ led to the separation of the churches in Mesopotamia from those of the Roman Empire; they would become known as the Church of the East.[7] Rivalry with Rome led the Sasanians to support the Church of the East, which flourished as a result. Arbela became the seat of a Metropolitan bishop and local Christian traditions found new roles for prominent figures and sites of Assyrian history. Here is one example:

> King Sennacherib had two children, Behnam and Sarah. One day, Behnam was out hunting with forty slaves and became separated from them. Spending the night alone in the wilderness, an angel appeared in a dream to Behnam and told him to find Saint Matthew the Hermit on Mount Alfaf (in northern Iraq), as he could heal Sarah, who was suffering from leprosy. The following day Behnam rejoined the slaves and together they discovered the hermit in a cave, who explained Christianity to the prince. Behnam was doubtful about the faith and so

Matthew told him to bring Sarah to him and the Saint healed her leprosy. Behnam, Sarah, and the forty slaves were then baptised with water from a spring that appeared miraculously when Matthew hit the ground with his staff. When, however, Sennacherib discovered that his children had become Christians he was enraged and threatened to punish them if they didn't abandon their new faith. Behnam, Sarah, and the forty slaves fled to Mount Alfaf, but were killed by the king's soldiers. The death of his children sent Sennacherib mad. An angel appeared to Behnam's mother and told her that the king would only be cured if he converted to Christianity and prayed at the site of the martyrs' death. Following the angel's advice, Sennacherib was freed of his madness and he and Behnam's mother were then baptised by Saint Matthew at Ashur. At the request of Saint Matthew, the king ordered the construction of a monastery on Mount Alfaf that exists to this day.[8]

From Mesopotamia to Iraq

Between 633 and 651, Arab armies, united under Islam, conquered the Sasanian Empire. Across the Tigris from the remains of Nineveh and the village of Nebi Yunus – where a church marked the supposed grave of the biblical prophet Jonah – a mosque was built as early as 642, around which would grow the city of Mosul. As a 'People of the Book', the Christian communities were permitted to practise their faith in exchange for loyalty and the payment of a tax. Arabic gradually became the main spoken language of the Middle East, but Aramaic remained a spoken, literary and liturgical language for local Christians. Over the following centuries, as these communities faced periods of suppression and persecution, some would come to adopt the term used in Syriac Aramaic writings to refer to Assyria as a general self-designation.

By the nineteenth century, the region of northern Mesopotamia contained a diverse population: Arabs with Assyrians, Armenians, Turkmens, Kurds, Yazidis, Shabakis, Mandaeans, Kawliya and Circassians. Some of these local people were employed by Europeans to uncover the monuments of ancient Assyria – and are

Photograph by Gabriel Tranchand of excavations at Khorsabad, 1852.

captured in their traditional clothing in the earliest photographs ever taken of an archaeological excavation. The French photographer Gabriel Tranchand took the image shown here at Khorsabad in 1852. Standing in a gateway beneath an arch of glazed bricks supported by a pair of *lamassus*, the crowd of men include individuals wearing the distinctive pointed headgear of local Christians.

The decline of the Ottoman Empire, which had dominated the Middle East for nearly four hundred years, exacerbated tensions between communities and there were massacres of minority groups, including Assyrians. By the end of the nineteenth century, the Assyrian Church of the East had come to represent a majority of Assyrians, which in turn led to the emergence of an Assyrian independence movement. In the aftermath of the First World War, however, when the Ottoman Empire was being carved up to form new nation states, the Assyrians were left out and many of them emigrated to the United States and South America. There remained, however, a number of Assyrian towns and villages in the north of the newly established Kingdom of Iraq, as well as significant Assyrian Aramaic-speaking communities in cities such as Mosul, Erbil, Kirkuk and Dohuk. These populations continued to suffer persecution in the volatile politics of the last century and were among the minority groups that faced the horrors of the Islamic State/Daesh occupation of northern Iraq between 2014 and 2017, which saw terrible atrocities to people alongside the attempted obliteration of their identity with the destruction of churches as well as attacks on ancient sites like Nimrud, Nineveh and Ashur.

In the face of such hostility the Assyrians have, however, retained a strong national and ethnic identity. So despite this book belonging to a series about 'lost civilizations', the Assyrians were never lost. As inhabitants of the land of Assyria and speaking a language that can be traced back to the empire itself, local people have claimed a local inheritance. Aspects of it are increasingly shared across Iraq – examples of guardian Assyrian *lamassus* can be found from Mosul to Basra as full-scale replicas, tourist souvenirs, artistic interpretations or protest graffiti, where they stand as symbols of liberation from the depredations of modern invaders and occupiers, but also as expressions of an immense pride in an ancient past that all communities can share.

REFERENCES

1 Ancient and Modern Empires

1 Austen Henry Layard, *Discoveries in the Ruins of Nineveh and Babylon, with Travels in Armenia, Kurdistan and the Desert* (London, 1853), p. 437.
2 Harput (Kharberd) is the modern town of Elâzığ, Turkey.
3 Horatio Southgate, *Narrative of a Visit to the Syrian Jacobite Church of Mesopotamia; with Statements and Reflections upon the Present State of Christianity in Turkey, and the Character and Prospects of the Eastern Churches* (New York, 1844), p. 80.
4 Austen Henry Layard, *Nineveh and Its Remains*, vol. I (London, 1949), p. 107.
5 Marcus N. Adler, *The Itinerary of Benjamin of Tudela: Critical Text, Translation and Commentary* (New York, 1907), pp. 33–4.
6 Claudius James Rich, *Narrative of a Residence in Kurdistan and on the Site of Ancient Nineveh*, vol. II (London, 1836), p. 131.
7 St John Simpson, 'From Persepolis to Babylon and Nineveh: The Rediscovery of the Ancient Near East', in *Enlightenment: Discovering the World in the Eighteenth Century*, ed. K. Sloan and A. Burnett (London, 2003), pp. 192–201.
8 Paul-Émile Botta and Eugène Flandin, *Les monuments de Ninive*, vols I–V (Paris, 1849–50).
9 Joseph Bonomi, *Nineveh and Its Palaces: The Discoveries of Botta and Layard, Applied to the Elucidation of Holy Writ* (London, 1875), p. 347.
10 Cyril J. Gadd, *The Stones of Assyria: The Surviving Remains of Assyrian Sculpture, Their Recovery and Their Original Positions* (London, 1936), pp. 160–63.
11 Bonomi, *Nineveh and Its Palaces*, p. 347.
12 Mogens Trolle Larsen, *The Conquest of Assyria: Excavations in an Antique Land* (London and New York, 1996), p. 96.
13 Paul Collins, 'From Mesopotamia to the Met: Two Assyrian Reliefs from the Palace of Sargon II', *Metropolitan Museum Journal*, XLVII (2012), pp. 73–84.
14 Frederick N. Bohrer, *Orientalism and Visual Culture: Imagining Mesopotamia in Nineteenth-Century Europe* (Cambridge, 2003), p. 121.

15 Gordon Loud, *Khorsabad*, Part 1: *Excavations in the Palace and at a City Gate* (Chicago, IL, 1936); John Malcolm Russell, *From Nineveh to New York: The Strange Story of the Assyrian Reliefs in the Metropolitan Museum and the Hidden Masterpiece at Canford School* (New Haven, CT, and London, 1997), p. 164.

2 Ancient Origins

1 Prudence O. Harper, Evelyn Klengel-Brandt, Joan Aruz and Kim Benzel, *Discoveries at Ashur on the Tigris: Assyrian Origins. Antiquities in the Vorderasiatisches Museum, Berlin* (New York, 1995).
2 Karen Radner, 'The Assur–Nineveh–Arbela Triangle: Central Assyria in the Neo-Assyrian Period', in *Between the Cultures: The Central Tigris Region in Mesopotamia from the 3rd to the 1st Millennium BC*, ed. P. Miglus and S. Mühl (Heidelberg, 2011), pp. 321–9.
3 David Wengrow, '"The Changing Face of Clay": Continuity and Change in the Transition from Village to Urban Life in the Near East', *Antiquity*, LXXII/278 (1998), pp. 783–95.
4 Marco Iamoni, 'The Prehistoric Roots of Nineveh', in *Nineveh: The Great City*, ed. L. P. Petit and D. Morandi Bonacossi (Leiden, 2017), p. 111.
5 Augusta McMahon, 'The Lion, the King and the Cage: Late Chalcolithic Iconography and Ideology in Northern Mesopotamia', *Iraq*, LXXI (2009), p. 117.
6 Guillermo Algaze, 'The End of Prehistory and the Uruk Period', in *The Sumerian World*, ed. H. Crawford (Abingdon and New York, 2013), pp. 68–94.
7 Julian E. Reade, 'The Ishtar Temple at Nineveh', *Iraq*, LXVII/1 (2005), pp. 347–90.
8 Inana may originally have been perceived as a separate goddess to the Semitic/Assyrian Ishtar; see Tzvi Abusch, 'Ištar', *Nin*, I (2000), pp. 23–7.
9 Gary Beckman, 'Ištar of Nineveh Reconsidered', *Journal of Cuneiform Studies*, L (1998), pp. 1–10.
10 Jean-Claude Margueron, *Mari, Capital of Northern Mesopotamia in the Third Millennium: The Archaeology of Tell Hariri on the Euphrates* (Oxford and Philadelphia, PA, 2004).
11 Philippa Browne, Alexander Sollee and Christina Tsouparopoulou, 'The Mesopotamian Temple of Ištar in Aššur', available at www.godscollections.org, accessed 3 September 2022.
12 Albert Kirk Grayson, *Assyrian Rulers of the Third and Second Millennium BC (to 1115 BC)* (Toronto, 1987), A.0.1001.1.
13 Ibid., A.0.1002.2001.
14 Max E. L. Mallowan, 'The Bronze Head of the Akkadian Period from Nineveh', *Iraq*, III (1936), pp. 104–10; Reade, 'The Ishtar Temple at Nineveh', pp. 358–9.
15 Piotr Steinkeller, 'Tiš-atal's Visit to Nippur', *NABU*, 15 (2007), p. 108.

3 Merchants and Kings

1 Mogens Trolle Larsen, *Ancient Kanesh: A Merchant Colony in Bronze Age Anatolia* (Cambridge, 2015).
2 Klaas R. Veenhof, 'The Old Assyrian Period (20th–18th Century BCE)', in *A Companion to Assyria*, ed. E. Frahm (New Haven, CT, 2017), p. 71.
3 Julian E. Reade, 'Das Kultrelief aus Assur: Glas, Ziegen, Zapfen und Wasser', *Mitteilungen der Deutschen Orient-Gesellschaft zu Berlin*, CXXXII (2000), pp. 105–12.
4 Ira Spar, *Cuneiform Texts in the Metropolitan Museum of Art*, vol. I: *Tablets, Cones, and Bricks of the Third and Second Millennium BC* (New York, 1988), pp. 118–19.
5 Cécile Michel, 'Women of Assur and Kanis', in *Anatolia's Prologue, Kultepe Kanesh Karum, Assyrians in Istanbul*, ed. F. Kulakoglu and S. Kangal (Kayseri, 2010), p. 130.
6 John M. Russell, 'Assyrian Cities and Architecture', in *A Companion to Assyria*, ed. Frahm, pp. 427–8.
7 Albert Kirk Grayson, *Assyrian Rulers of the Third and Second Millennium BC (to 1115 BC)* (Toronto, 1987), A.0.39.2, ii.11.
8 Diana L. Stein, 'A Reappraisal of the "Sauštatar Letter" from Nuzi', *Zeitschrift für Assyriologie*, LXXXIV/1 (1989), pp. 11–37.
9 Amanda H. Podany, *Brotherhood of Kings* (New York, 2010).
10 Spar, *Cuneiform Texts*, no. 102, p. 149.
11 Albert Kirk Grayson, *Assyrian Royal Inscriptions I* (Wiesbaden, 1972), p. 48.
12 Oscar W. Muscarella, *Bronze and Iron: Ancient Near Eastern Artifacts in the Metropolitan Museum of Art* (New York, 1988), p. 340, no. 472.
13 The ancient term 'black-headed' referred to the population of Mesopotamia, if not the world. See Grayson, *Assyrian Rulers of the Third and Second Millennium BC*, A.0.77.1:22–6.
14 Ibid., A.0.78.23:60–8.
15 Zainab Bahrani, *The Graven Image: Representation in Babylonia and Assyria* (Philadelphia, PA, 2003), pp. 192–8.
16 Grayson, *Assyrian Rulers of the Third and Second Millennium BC*, A.0.78.23, lines 92–108.
17 Albert Kirk Grayson, *Assyrian Rulers of the Early First Millennium BC*, Part I *(1114–859 BC)* (Toronto, 1991), A.0.87.10, line 77.

4 The Assyrian Empire

1 Albert Kirk Grayson, *Assyrian Rulers of the Early First Millennium BC*, Part I *(1114–859 BC)* (Toronto, 1991), A.0.101.30, lines 1, 21–7.
2 Joan Oates and David Oates, *Nimrud: An Assyrian Imperial City Revealed* (London, 2001), pp. 40–42.
3 Grayson, *Rulers of the Early First Millennium BC*, Part I, A.0.101.1, lines iii, 64b–69b.

4 For the date of the palace see Nicolò Marchetti, 'Texts Quoting Artworks: The Banquet Stele and the Palace Reliefs of Assurnasirpal II', *Revue d'assyriologie et d'archéologie orientale*, CIII/1 (2009), pp. 85–90 (p. 85).
5 Max E. L. Mallowan, *Nimrud and Its Remains* (London, 1966).
6 Ludovico Portuese, *Life at Court: Ideology and Audience in the Late Assyrian Palace* (Münster, 2020).
7 David Kertai, *The Architecture of Late Assyrian Royal Palaces* (Oxford, 2015), p. 10.
8 Ibid., p. 30.
9 Shiyanthi Thavapalan, 'A World in Color: Polychromy of Assyrian Sculpture', in *Ancient Mesopotamia Speaks: Highlights of the Yale Babylonian Collection*, ed. A. Lassen, E. Frahm and K. Wagensonner (New Haven, CT, 2019), pp. 193–200.
10 Marchetti, 'Texts Quoting Artworks', p. 86.
11 Paul Collins, 'Kingship in Time and Space in the Northwest Palace, Nimrud', in *Near Eastern Weltanschauungen in Contact and in Contrast: Rethinking Ideology and Propaganda in the Ancient Near East*, ed. L. Portuese and M. Pallavidini (Münster, 2022), pp. 183–204.
12 Grayson, *Rulers of the Early First Millennium BC*, Part I, A.0.101.30, lines 102–54.
13 Erle Leichty, *The Royal Inscriptions of Esarhaddon, King of Assyria (680–669 BC)* (Winona Lake, IN, 2011), no. 1, lines ii.30–39.
14 Beate Pongratz-Leisten, *Religion and Ideology in Assyria* (Munich and Boston, MA, 2015), pp. 435–41.
15 Simo Parpola, *Assyrian Royal Rituals and Cultic Texts* (Helsinki, 2017), no. 7, lines i.26–9.
16 Ibid., lines ii.30–36.
17 Simo Parpola, *Assyrian Royal Rituals and Cultic Texts: Letters from Assyrian and Babylonian Scholars* (Helsinki, 1993), no. 185, lines 7–9.
18 The lists were perhaps first composed in the fourteenth century BC. See Jonathan Valk, 'The Origins of the Assyrian King List', *Journal of Ancient Near Eastern History*, VI/1 (2019), pp. 1–17.
19 David Kertei, 'The Iconography of the Late Assyrian Crown Prince', in *From the Four Corners of the Earth: Studies in the Iconography and Cultures of the Ancient Near East in Honour of F.A.M. Wiggermann*, ed. D. Kertai and O. Nieuwenhuyse (Münster, 2017), pp. 111–33.
20 Karen Radner, 'Revolts in the Assyrian Empire: Succession Wars, Rebellions against a False King and Independence Movements', in *Revolt and Resistance in the Ancient Classical World and the Near East: In the Crucible of Empire*, ed. J. J. Collins and J. G. Manning (Leiden, 2016), p. 47.
21 Annie Caubet, ed., *Khorsabad, le palais de Sargon II, roi d'Assyrie* (Paris, 1995).
22 Simo Parpola, *The Correspondence of Sargon II*, Part I: *Letters from Assyria and the West* (Helsinki, 1987), no. 33, lines 1–18.
23 Ibid., no. 31, lines OBV 21–REV 3.
24 Leichty, *The Royal Inscriptions of Esarhaddon*, no. 1, lines i.43–4.

25 Stephanie M. Dalley and Luis R. Siddall, 'A Conspiracy to Murder Sennacherib? A Revision of SAA 18 100 in the Light of a Recent Join', *Iraq*, LXXXIII (2021), pp. 45–56.

26 Albert Kirk Grayson, *Assyrian and Babylonian Chronicles* (Locust Valley, NY, 1975), Chronicle 1, lines iii.34–5.

27 Simo Parpola and Kazuko Watanabe, *Neo-Assyrian Treaties and Loyalty Oaths* (Helsinki, 1988), no. 6, lines 41–62.

28 Ibid., lines 414–72.

29 Ibid., lines i–iv.

30 Andrew R. George, 'Sennacherib and the Tablet of Destinies', *Iraq*, XLVIII (1986), pp. 133–46.

31 Parpola and Watanabe, *Neo-Assyrian Treaties and Loyalty Oaths*, no. 6, lines 664–70.

32 Karen Radner, 'The Trials of Esarhaddon: The Conspiracy of 670 BC', *ISIMU*, VI (2003), pp. 165–84 (p. 172).

33 Albert Kirk Grayson, *Assyrian Rulers of the Early First Millennium* BC, Part II *(858–745* BC*)* (Toronto, 1996), A.0.104.2001.

34 Saana Svärd, *Women and Power in Neo-Assyrian Palaces* (Helsinki, 2015), p. 40.

35 As Semiramis she would be the inspiration for classical authors. See Henrietta McCall, 'Recovery and Aftermath', in *The Legacy of Mesopotamia*, ed. S. Dalley (Oxford, 1998), pp. 183–213.

36 Grayson, *Rulers of the Early First Millennium* BC, Part II *(858–745* BC*)*, A.0.104.1.

37 Ibid., A.0.104.2002, line 8b.

38 Sherry L. Macgregor, *Beyond Hearth and Home: Women in the Public Sphere in Neo-Assyrian Society* (Helsinki, 2012), p. 80.

39 Muzahim M. Hussein, *Nimrud: The Queens' Tombs*, trans. Mark Altaweel (Chicago, IL, 2016).

40 Farouk N. H. Al-Rawi, 'Inscriptions from the Tombs of the Queens of Assyria', in *New Light on Nimrud: Proceedings of the Nimrud Conference, 11th–13th March 2002*, ed. J. E. Curtis, H. McCall, D. Collon and L. al-Gailani Werr (London, 2008), pp. 123–4.

41 Stephanie Dalley, 'The Identity of the Princesses in Tomb II and a New Analysis of Events in 701 BC', in *New Light on Nimrud*, p. 171.

42 Michael Müller-Karpe, Manfred Kunter and Michael Schultz, 'Results of the Palaeopathological Investigations on the Royal Skeletons from Nimrud', in *New Light on Nimrud*, p. 144.

43 Sväd, *Women and Power*, p. 52.

44 Amy Gansell, 'Dressing the Neo-Assyrian Queen in Identity and Ideology: Elements and Ensembles from the Royal Tombs at Nimrud', *American Journal of Archaeology*, CXXII (2018), pp. 65–100; Amy Gansell, 'Images and Conceptions of Ideal Feminine Beauty in Neo-Assyrian Royal Context, ca. 883–627 BCE', in *Critical Approaches to Ancient Near Eastern Art*, ed. M. Feldman and B. Brown (Boston, MA, 2013), pp. 391–420.

45 Steven W. Cole and Peter Machinist, *Letters from Priests to the Kings Esarhaddon and Assurbanipal* (Helsinki, 1998), no. 61.

46 Parpola and Watanabe, *Neo-Assyrian Treaties and Loyalty Oaths*, no. 8, lines 9–15, r18–r27.

47 Mikko Luukko and Greta van Buylaere, *The Political Correspondence of Esarhaddon* (Helsinki, 2002), no. 28.

48 Karen Radner, 'After Eltekeh: Royal Hostages from Egypt at the Assyrian Court', in *Stories of Long Ago: Festschrift für Michael D. Roaf*, ed. H. Baker, K. Kaniuth and A. Otton (Münster, 2012), pp. 471–9.

49 Hayim Tadmor and Shigeo Yamada, *The Royal Inscriptions of Tiglath-pileser III (744–727 BC) and Shalmaneser V (726–722 BC), Kings of Assyria* (Winona Lake, IN, 2011), Tiglath-pileser III composite annals, Fragment 2, lines 3 and 11b.

50 Karen Radner, 'Running the Empire: Assyrian Governance', *Assyrian Empire Builders*, University College London, 2021, http://oracc.museum.upenn.edu, accessed 1 December 2022. Raija Mattila, *The King's Magnates: A Study of the Highest Officials of the Neo-Assyrian Empire* (Helsinki, 2000).

51 Paul Collins, 'Attending the King in the Assyrian Reliefs', in *Assyrian Reliefs from the Palace of Ashurnasirpal II: A Cultural Biography*, ed. A. Cohen and S. E. Kangas (Hanover, NH, and London, 2010), pp. 181–97.

52 Davide Nadali, 'Neo-Assyrian State Seals: An Allegory of Power', *State Archives of Assyria Bulletin*, XVIII (2011), pp. 215–43; Karen Radner, 'The Delegation of Power: Neo-Assyrian Bureau Seals', in *L'archive des fortifications de Persépolis: État des questions et perspectives de recherches*, ed. P. Briant et al. (Paris, 2008), pp. 481–515.

53 Karen Radner, 'An Imperial Communication Network: The State Correspondence of the Neo-Assyrian Empire', in *State Correspondence in the Ancient World: From New Kingdom Egypt to the Roman Empire*, ed. K. Radner (Oxford, 2014), pp. 64–93.

54 Manfried Dietrich, *The Neo-Babylonian Correspondence of Sargon and Sennacherib* (Helsinki, 2003), no. 2, lines 15–21.

55 Grant Frame, *The Royal Inscriptions of Sargon II, King of Assyria (721–705 BC)* (Winona Lake, IN, 2021), no. 1, lines 62–5.

56 Tamás Dezső: *The Assyrian Army*, vol. I (2 parts): *The Structure of the Neo-Assyrian Army. 1. Infantry 2. Cavalry and Chariotry* (Budapest, 2012).

57 Davide Nadali, 'Images of Assyrian Sieges: What They Show, What We Know, What We Can Say', in *Brill's Companion to Sieges in the Ancient Mediterranean*, ed. J. Armstrong and M. Trundle (Leiden and Boston, MA, 2019), pp. 53–68.

58 Karen Radner, 'High Visibility Punishment and Deterrent: Impalement in Assyrian Warfare and Legal Practice', *Zeitschrift für Altorientalische und Biblische Rechtsgeschichte*, XXI (2015), p. 105.

59 Davide Nadali, 'The Representations of Foreign Soldiers and Their Employment in the Assyrian Army', in *Ethnicity in Ancient Mesopotamia*, ed. W. H. van Soldt (Leiden, 2005), pp. 222–44.

60 Davide Nadali, 'Outcomes of Battle: Triumphal Celebrations in Assyria', in *Rituals of Triumph in the Mediterranean World*, ed. A. Spalinger and J. Armstrong (Leiden, 2013), pp. 75–94.
61 Jamie Novotny and Joshua Jeffers, *The Royal Inscriptions of Ashurbanipal (668–631 BC), Assur-etal-ilani (630–627 BC), and Sin-sarra-iskun (626–612 BC), Kings of Assyria*, Part I (University Park, PA, 2018), no. 4, lines vi 77–95.
62 Tadmor and Yamada, *The Royal Inscriptions of Tiglath-pileser III*, no. 47, lines 1–2.
63 Yervand Grekyan, 'The Kingdom of Urartu', in *The Oxford History of the Ancient Near East*, vol. IV: *The Age of Assyria*, ed. K. Radner, N. Moeller and D. T. Potts (New York, 2023), online edn, https://doi.org/10.1093/oso/9780190687632.003.0044, accessed 30 March 2023.
64 Karen Radner, 'Assyria and the Medes', in *The Oxford Handbook of Ancient Iran*, ed. D. T. Potts (Oxford, 2013), pp. 442–56.
65 Daniel T. Potts, *The Archaeology of Elam* (Cambridge, 2016).
66 Geoff Emberling, 'Kush under the Dynasty of Napata', in *The Oxford History of the Ancient Near East*, vol. IV: *The Age of Assyria*.
67 Grayson, *Assyrian Rulers of the Early First Millennium BC*, Part II, A.0.102.2, lines ii.90b–94b
68 Tadmor and Yamada, *The Royal Inscriptions of Tiglath-pileser III*, no. 44, lines 17–18.
69 Françoise Briquel Chatonnet, 'The Iron Age States on the Phoenician Coast', in *The Oxford History of the Ancient Near East*, vol. IV: *The Age of Assyria*, pp. 1027–114 (print edn).
70 Mikko Luukko, *The Correspondence of Tiglath-Pileser III and Sargon II from Calah/Nimrud* (Helsinki, 2012), no. 147, line r19.
71 Karen Radner, 'Assyrian Imperial Power and How to Oppose It', The Institute for the Study of Ancient Cultures, University of Chicago, lecture delivered 1 May 2019, www.youtube.com, accessed 1 December 2021.
72 Albert Kirk Grayson and Jamie Novotny, *The Royal Inscriptions of Sennacherib, King of Assyria (704–681 BC)*, Part I (Winona Lake, IN, 2012), no. 2, lines 46–7.
73 Ibid., no. 4, lines 49–51.
74 Yosef Garfinkel, Jon W. Carroll, Michael Pytlik and Madeleine Mumcuoglu, 'Constructing the Assyrian Siege Ramp at Lachish: Texts, Iconography, Archaeology and Photogrammetry', *Oxford Journal of Archaeology*, XL/4 (2021), pp. 417–39.
75 Grayson and Novotny, *Inscriptions of Sennacherib*, Part I, no. 4, lines 55–8.
76 Ibid., no. 22, lines v.35–6.
77 Ibid., lines v.74–79, vi.2.
78 Ibid., no. 223, lines 50b–53b.
79 Parpola, *The Correspondence of Sargon II*, Part I, no. 177, lines 4–16.
80 Albert Kirk Grayson and Jamie Novotny, *The Royal Inscriptions of Sennacherib, King of Assyria (704–681 BC)*, Part II (Winona Lake, IN, 2014), no. 61.

81 Karen Radner, 'Mass Deportation: The Assyrian Resettlement Policy', *Assyrian Empire Builders*, University College London, 2021, http://oracc.museum.upenn.edu, accessed 18 June 2021.
82 Bustenay Oded, *Mass Deportations and Deportees in the Neo-Assyrian Empire* (Wiesbaden, 1979).
83 Leichty, *The Royal Inscriptions of Esarhaddon*, Part 1, no. 1, lines vi.35–43.
84 Kertai, *The Architecture of Late Assyrian Royal Palaces*, p. 121.
85 Grayson and Novotny, *Inscriptions of Sennacherib*, no. 16, lines v.57–70; vi.53–7; vii.17–21; viii.12–23.
86 Daniele Morandi Bonacossi, 'The Creation of the Assyrian Heartland: New Data from the "Land behind Nineveh"', in *The Archaeology of Imperial Landscape: A Comparative Study of Empires in the Ancient Near East and Mediterranean World*, ed. B. S. Düring and T. Stek (Cambridge, 2018), pp. 48–85.
87 Thorkild Jacobsen and Seton Lloyd, *Sennacherib's Aqueduct at Jerwan* (Chicago, IL, 1935).
88 Parpola, *Letters from Assyrian and Babylonian Scholars*, no. 315, lines 7–10; 20–r3.
89 Karen Radner, 'Royal Decision-Making: Kings, Magnates and Scholars', in *The Oxford Handbook of Cuneiform Culture*, ed. K. Radner and E. Robson (Oxford, 2011), pp. 358–79.
90 Eleanor Robson, *Ancient Knowledge Networks: A Social Geography of Cuneiform Scholarship in First-Millennium Assyria and Babylonia* (London, 2019).
91 Troels Pank Arbøll, *Medicine in Ancient Assur: A Microhistorical Study of the Neo-Assyrian Healer Kisir-Aššur* (Leiden and Boston, MA, 2019).
92 Moudhy Al-Rashid, 'Roaming, Malicious, Hooligan Ghosts', *London Review of Books*, XLIV/2 (2022), www.lrb.co.uk, accessed 15 July 2023.
93 Marc van de Mieroop, *Philosophy Before the Greeks: The Pursuit of Truth in Ancient Babylonia* (Princeton, NJ, 2016), p. 96.
94 Radner, 'The Trials of Esarhaddon', p. 169.
95 Jeremy Black and Anthony Green, *Gods, Demons and Symbols of Ancient Mesopotamia: An Illustrated Dictionary* (London, 1992), pp. 115–16; Frans A. M. Wiggermann, 'Lamaštu, Daughter of Anu: A Profile', in *Birth in Babylonia and the Bible: Its Mediterranean Setting*, ed. M. Stol (Groningen, 2000), pp. 217–52.
96 Nils P. Heeßel, 'Evil against Evil: The Demon Pazuzu', *Studi e Materiali di Storia delle Religioni*, LXXVII/2 (2011), pp. 357–68.
97 Van de Mieroop, *Philosophy Before the Greeks*, p. 93.
98 Ivan Starr, *Queries to the Sungod: Divination and Politics in Sargonid Assyria* (Helsinki, 1990), no. 20, lines 4–7.
99 Radner, 'The Trials of Esarhaddon', pp. 171–2.
100 Parpola, *Letters from Assyrian and Babylonian Scholars*, no. 352, lines obv. 1–21.
101 Robson, *Ancient Knowledge Networks*, p. 68.

102 A. Leo Oppenheim, 'The City of Assur in 714 B.C.', *Journal of Near Eastern Studies*, XIX/2 (1960), pp. 133–47 (pp. 136–8).
103 Grayson and Novotny, *Inscriptions of Sennacherib*, Part I, no. 17, lines vi.80–85; vi.89–vii.8.
104 Jonathan Taylor, 'Knowledge: The Key to Assyrian Power', in *I Am Ashurbanipal: King of the World, King of Assyria*, ed. G. Brereton (London, 2018), pp. 93–4.
105 Jamie Novotny and Joshua Jeffers, *Inscriptions of Ashurbanipal*, no. 220, lines i.13–18.
106 Robson, *Ancient Knowledge Networks*, pp. 126–7, 264.
107 Grayson and Novotny, *Inscriptions of Sennacherib*, Part I, no. 1, line 86.
108 Cole and Machinist, *Letters from Priests*, no. 34, lines 11–23.
109 Novotny and Jeffers, *Inscriptions of Ashurbanipal*, Part I, no. 3, line viii.65
110 Ibid., no. 3, lines i.60–64.
111 Ibid., no. 3, lines i.65–81b.
112 Ibid., no. 3, lines ii.12–37.
113 Ibid., no. 3, lines v.24b–27b; v.51b–55b.
114 Ibid., no. 3, lines 56b–72b.
115 Ronnie Goldstein and Elnathan Weissert, 'The Battle of Til-Tuba Cycle and the Documentary Evidence', in *I Am Ashurbanipal: King of the World, King of Assyria*, pp. 248–68.
116 Novotny and Jeffers, *Inscriptions of Ashurbanipal*, Part I, no. 3, line iii.70.
117 Ibid., no. 3, line iii.107.
118 Ibid., no. 3, line iv.46.
119 Elnathan Weissert, 'Royal Hunt and Royal Triumph in a Prism Fragment of Assurbanipal', in *ASSYRIA 1995: Proceedings of the 10th Anniversary Symposium of the Neo-Assyrian Text Corpus Project, Helsinki, September 7–11*, ed. S. Parpola and R. M. Whiting (Helsinki, 1995), pp. 339–58.
120 Paul Collins, 'Trees and Gender in Assyrian Art', *Iraq*, LXVIII (2006), pp. 99–107 (p. 102).
121 Diana Pickworth, 'Excavations at Nineveh: The Halzi Gate', *Iraq*, LXVII/1 (2005), pp. 295–316.
122 St John Simpson, 'Annihilating Assyria', in *In Context: The Reade Festschrift*, ed. I. L. Finkel and St J. Simpson (Oxford, 2020), pp. 141–68.
123 Paul Collins, 'Some Thoughts on the Assyrian Ivories from the Temple of Nabu at Nimrud', in *Ivories, Rock Reliefs and Merv: Studies on the Ancient Near East in Honour of Georgina Herrmann*, ed. D. Wicke and J. Curtis (Münster, 2022), pp. 69–82.
124 Karen Radner, 'Last Emperor or Crown Prince Forever? Aššur-uballiṭ II of Assyria According to Archival Sources', *State Archives of Assyria Studies*, XXVIII (2019), pp. 135–42.

125 Timothy Matney, John MacGinnis, Dirk Wicke and Kemalettin Koroglu, *Ziyaret Tepe: Exploring the Anatolian Frontier of the Assyrian Empire* (Edinburgh, 2017).

126 Simo Parpola, 'Cuneiform Texts from Ziyaret Tepe (Tushan), 2002–2003', *State Archives of Assyria Bulletin*, XVII (2008), pp. 1–113 (p. 88).

5 The Aftermath of Empire

1 Michael Roaf, 'Cyaxares in Assyria', *NABU*, 4 (2021), pp. 277–9.

2 Irving Finkel, 'The Cyrus Cylinder: The Babylonian Perspective', in *The Cyrus Cylinder: The King of Persia's Proclamation from Ancient Babylon*, ed. I. Finkel (London, 2013), pp. 6–7.

3 Karen Radner, 'Assur's "Second Temple Period": The Restoration of the Cult of Aššur, c. 538 BC', in *Herrschaftslegitimation in vorderorientalischen Reichen der Eisenzeit*, ed. C. Levin and R. Müller (Tübingen, 2017), pp. 77–96.

4 Alison Salvesen, 'The Legacy of Babylon and Nineveh in Aramaic Sources', in *The Legacy of Mesopotamia*, ed. S. Dalley (Oxford, 1998), pp. 139–62.

5 Richard C. Steiner and Charles F. Nims, 'Ashurbanipal and Shamash-shum-ukin: A Tale of Two Brothers from the Aramaic Text in Demotic Script. Part 1', *Revue biblique (1946–)*, XCII/1 (1985), pp. 60–81.

6 Stefan R. Hauser, 'Post-Imperial Assyria', in *A Companion to Assyria*, ed. E. Frahm (Hoboken, NJ, 2017), pp. 229–46.

7 Christoph Baumer, *The Church of the East: An Illustrated History of Assyrian Christianity* (London, 2006).

8 Jeanne-Nicole Mellon Saint-Laurent and Kyle Smith, eds, *The History of Mar Behnam and Sarah: Martyrdom and Monasticism in Medieval Iraq* (Piscataway, NJ, 2018).

BIBLIOGRAPHY

Abusch, Tzvi, 'Ištar', *Nin*, I (2000), pp. 23–7

Adler, Marcus N., *The Itinerary of Benjamin of Tudela: Critical Text, Translation and Commentary* (New York, 1907)

Algaze, Guillermo, 'The End of Prehistory and the Uruk Period', in *The Sumerian World*, ed. H. Crawford (Abingdon and New York, 2013), pp. 68–94

Al-Rashid, Moudhy, 'Roaming, Malicious, Hooligan Ghosts', *London Review of Books* XLIV/2 (2022), www.lrb.co.uk

Al-Rawi, Farouk N. H., 'Inscriptions from the Tombs of the Queens of Assyria', in *New Light on Nimrud: Proceedings of the Nimrud Conference 11th–13th March 2002*, ed. J. E. Curtis, H. McCall, D. Collon and L. al-Gailani Werr (London, 2008), pp. 119–38

Arbøll, Troels Pank, *Medicine in Ancient Assur: A Microhistorical Study of the Neo-Assyrian Healer Kisir-Aššur* (Leiden and Boston, MA, 2019)

Bahrani, Zainab, *The Graven Image: Representation in Babylonia and Assyria* (Philadelphia, PA, 2003)

Baumer, Christoph, *The Church of the East: An Illustrated History of Assyrian Christianity* (London, 2006)

Beckman, Gary, 'Ištar of Nineveh Reconsidered', *Journal of Cuneiform Studies*, L (1998), pp. 1–10

Black, Jeremy, and Anthony Green, *Gods, Demons and Symbols of Ancient Mesopotamia: An Illustrated Dictionary* (London, 1992)

Bohrer, Frederick N., *Orientalism and Visual Culture: Imagining Mesopotamia in Nineteenth-Century Europe* (Cambridge, 2003)

Bonomi, Joseph, *Nineveh and Its Palaces: The Discoveries of Botta and Layard, Applied to the Elucidation of Holy Writ* (London, 1875)

Botta, Paul-Émile, and Eugène Flandin, *Les monuments de Ninive*, vols I–V (Paris, 1849–50)

Browne, Philippa, Alexander Sollee and Christina Tsouparopoulou, 'The Mesopotamian Temple of Ištar in Aššur', www.godscollections.org

Bustenay, Oded, *Mass Deportations and Deportees in the Neo-Assyrian Empire* (Wiesbaden, 1979)

Caubet, Annie, ed., *Khorsabad, le palais de Sargon II, roi d'Assyrie* (Paris, 1995)
Chatonnet, Françoise Briquel, 'The Iron Age States on the Phoenician Coast', in *The Oxford History of the Ancient Near East*, vol. IV: *The Age of Assyria*, ed. K. Radner, N. Moeller and D. T. Potts (New York, 2023), pp. 1027–114
Cole, Steven W., and Peter Machinist, *Letters from Priests to the Kings Esarhaddon and Assurbanipal* (Helsinki, 1998)
Collins, Paul, 'Trees and Gender in Assyrian Art', *Iraq*, LXVIII (2006), pp. 99–107
—, 'Attending the King in the Assyrian Reliefs', in *Assyrian Reliefs from the Palace of Ashurnasirpal II: A Cultural Biography*, ed. A. Cohen and S. E. Kangas (Hanover, NH, and London, 2010), pp. 181–97
—, 'From Mesopotamia to the Met: Two Assyrian Reliefs from the Palace of Sargon II', *Metropolitan Museum Journal*, XLVII (2012), pp. 73–84
—, 'Kingship in Time and Space in the Northwest Palace, Nimrud', in *Near Eastern Weltanschauungen in Contact and in Contrast: Rethinking Ideology and Propaganda in the Ancient Near East*, ed. L. Portuese and M. Pallavidini (Münster, 2022), pp. 183–204
—, 'Some Thoughts on the Assyrian Ivories from the Temple of Nabu at Nimrud', in *Ivories, Rock Reliefs and Merv: Studies on the Ancient Near East in Honour of Georgina Herrmann*, ed. D. Wicke and J. Curtis (Münster, 2022), pp. 69–82
Dalley, Stephanie, 'The Identity of the Princesses in Tomb II and a New Analysis of Events in 701 BC', in *New Light on Nimrud: Proceedings of the Nimrud Conference 11th–13th March 2002*, ed. J. E. Curtis, H. McCall, D. Collon and L. al-Gailani Werr (London, 2008), pp. 171–5
Dalley, Stephanie M., and Luis R. Siddall, 'A Conspiracy to Murder Sennacherib? A Revision of SAA 18 100 in the Light of a Recent Join', *Iraq*, LXXXIII (2021), pp. 45–56
Dezső, Tamás: *The Assyrian Army* I/1–2. *The Structure of the Neo-Assyrian Army. 1. Infantry 2. Cavalry and Chariotry* (Budapest, 2012)
Dietrich, Manfried, *The Neo-Babylonian Correspondence of Sargon and Sennacherib* (Helsinki, 2003)
Emberling, Geoff, 'Kush under the Dynasty of Napata', in *The Oxford History of the Ancient Near East*, vol. IV: *The Age of Assyria*, ed. K. Radner, N. Moeller and D. T. Potts (New York, 2023), online edn
Finkel, Irving, 'The Cyrus Cylinder: The Babylonian Perspective', in *The Cyrus Cylinder: The King of Persia's Proclamation from Ancient Babylon*, ed. I. Finkel (London, 2013), pp. 4–34
Frame, Grant, *The Royal Inscriptions of Sargon II, King of Assyria (721–705 BC)* (Winona Lake, IN, 2021)
Gadd, Cyril J., *The Stones of Assyria: The Surviving Remains of Assyrian Sculpture, Their Recovery and Their Original Positions* (London, 1936)
Gansell, Amy, 'Images and Conceptions of Ideal Feminine Beauty in Neo-Assyrian Royal Context, ca. 883–627 BCE', in *Critical Approaches to Ancient Near Eastern Art*, ed. M. Feldman and B. Brown (Boston, MA, 2013), pp. 391–420

—, 'Dressing the Neo-Assyrian Queen in Identity and Ideology: Elements and Ensembles from the Royal Tombs at Nimrud', *American Journal of Archaeology*, CXXII (2018), pp. 65–100

Garfinkel, Yosef, Jon W. Carroll, Michael Pytlik and Madeleine Mumcuoglu, 'Constructing the Assyrian Siege Ramp at Lachish: Texts, Iconography, Archaeology and Photogrammetry', *Oxford Journal of Archaeology*, XL/4 (2021), pp. 417–39

George, Andrew R., 'Sennacherib and the Tablet of Destinies', *Iraq*, XLVIII (1986), pp. 133–46

Goldstein, Ronnie, and Elnathan Weissert, 'The Battle of Til-Tuba Cycle and the Documentary Evidence', in *I Am Ashurbanipal: King of the World, King of Assyria*, ed. G. Brereton (London, 2018), pp. 244–73

Grayson, Albert Kirk, *Assyrian Royal Inscriptions I* (Wiesbaden, 1972)

—, *Assyrian and Babylonian Chronicles* (Locust Valley, NY, 1975)

—, *Assyrian Rulers of the Third and Second Millennium BC (to 1115 BC)* (Toronto, 1987)

—, *Assyrian Rulers of the Early First Millennium BC*, Part I *(1114–859 BC)* (Toronto, 1991)

—, *Assyrian Rulers of the Early First Millennium BC*, Part II *(858–745 BC)* (Toronto, 1996)

Grayson, Albert Kirk, and Jamie Novotny, *The Royal Inscriptions of Sennacherib, King of Assyria (704–681 BC)*, Part I (Winona Lake, IN, 2012)

—, and —, *The Royal Inscriptions of Sennacherib, King of Assyria (704–681 BC)*, Part II (Winona Lake, IN, 2014)

Grekyan, Yervand, 'The Kingdom of Urartu', in *The Oxford History of the Ancient Near East*, vol. IV: *The Age of Assyria*, ed. K. Radner, N. Moeller and D. T. Potts (New York, 2023), online edn

Harper, Prudence O., Evelyn Klengel-Brandt, Joan Aruz and Kim Benzel, *Discoveries at Ashur on the Tigris: Assyrian Origins. Antiquities in the Vorderasiatisches Museum, Berlin* (New York, 1995)

Hauser, Stefan R., 'Post-Imperial Assyria', in *A Companion to Assyria*, ed. E. Frahm (Hoboken, NJ, 2017), pp. 229–46

Heeßel, Nils P., 'Evil against Evil: The Demon Pazuzu', *Studi e Materiali di Storia delle Religioni*, LXXVII/2 (2011), pp. 357–68

Hussein, Muzahim M., *Nimrud: The Queens' Tombs*, trans. Mark Altaweel (Chicago, IL, 2016)

Iamoni, Marco, 'The Prehistoric Roots of Nineveh', in *Nineveh: The Great City*, ed. L. P. Petit and D. Morandi Bonacossi (Leiden, 2017), pp. 109–12

Jacobsen, Thorkild, and Seton Lloyd, *Sennacherib's Aqueduct at Jerwan* (Chicago, IL, 1935)

Kertai, David, *The Architecture of Late Assyrian Royal Palaces* (Oxford, 2015)

—, 'The Iconography of the Late Assyrian Crown Prince', in *From the Four Corners of the Earth: Studies in the Iconography and Cultures of the Ancient Near East in Honour of F.A.M. Wiggermann*, ed. D. Kertai and O. Nieuwenhuyse (Münster, 2017), pp. 111–33

Larsen, Mogens Trolle, *The Conquest of Assyria: Excavations in an Antique Land* (London and New York, 1996)

—, *Ancient Kanesh: A Merchant Colony in Bronze Age Anatolia* (Cambridge, 2015)

Layard, Austen Henry, *Discoveries in the Ruins of Nineveh and Babylon, with Travels in Armenia, Kurdistan and the Desert* (London, 1853)

—, *Nineveh and Its Remains*, vol. I (London, 1949)

Leichty, Erle, *The Royal Inscriptions of Esarhaddon, King of Assyria (680–669 BC)* (Winona Lake, IN, 2011)

Loud, Gordon, *Khorsabad*, Part I: *Excavations in the Palace and at a City Gate* (Chicago, IL, 1936)

Luukko, Mikko, *The Correspondence of Tiglath-Pileser III and Sargon II from Calah/Nimrud* (Helsinki, 2012)

Luukko, Mikko, and Greta van Buylaere, *The Political Correspondence of Esarhaddon* (Helsinki, 2002)

McCall, Henrietta, 'Recovery and Aftermath', in *The Legacy of Mesopotamia*, ed. S. Dalley (Oxford, 1998), pp. 183–213

Macgregor, Sherry L., *Beyond Hearth and Home: Women in the Public Sphere in Neo-Assyrian Society* (Helsinki, 2012)

McMahon, Augusta, 'The Lion, the King and the Cage: Late Chalcolithic Iconography and Ideology in Northern Mesopotamia', *Iraq*, LXXI (2009), pp. 115–24

Mallowan, Max E. L., 'The Bronze Head of the Akkadian Period from Nineveh', *Iraq*, III (1936), pp. 104–10

—, *Nimrud and Its Remains*, vols I–II (London, 1966)

Marchetti, Nicolò, 'Texts Quoting Artworks: The Banquet Stele and the Palace Reliefs of Assurnasirpal II', *Revue d'assyriologie et d'archéologie orientale*, CIII/1 (2009), pp. 85–90

Margueron, Jean-Claude, *Mari, Capital of Northern Mesopotamia in the Third Millennium: The Archaeology of Tell Hariri on the Euphrates* (Oxford and Philadelphia, PA, 2004)

Matney, Timothy, John MacGinnis, Dirk Wicke and Kemalettin Koroglu, *Ziyaret Tepe: Exploring the Anatolian Frontier of the Assyrian Empire* (Edinburgh, 2017)

Mattila, Raija, *The King's Magnates: A Study of the Highest Officials of the Neo-Assyrian Empire* (Helsinki, 2000)

Michel, Cécile, 'Women of Assur and Kanis', in *Anatolia's Prologue, Kultepe Kanesh Karum, Assyrians in Istanbul*, ed. F. Kulakoglu and S. Kangal (Kayseri, 2010), pp. 124–33

Morandi Bonacossi, Daniele, 'The Creation of the Assyrian Heartland: New Data from the "Land behind Nineveh"', in *The Archaeology of Imperial Landscape: A Comparative Study of Empires in the Ancient Near East and Mediterranean World*, ed. B. S. Düring and T. Stek (Cambridge, 2018), pp. 48–85

Müller-Karpe, Michael, Manfred Kunter and Michael Schultz, 'Results of the Palaeopathological Investigations on the Royal Skeletons from Nimrud', in *New Light on Nimrud: Proceedings of the Nimrud Conference 11th–13th March 2002*, ed. J. E. Curtis, H. McCall, D. Collon and L. al-Gailani Werr (London, 2008), pp. 141–8

Muscarella, Oscar W., *Bronze and Iron: Ancient Near Eastern Artifacts in the Metropolitan Museum of Art* (New York, 1988)

Nadali, Davide, 'The Representations of Foreign Soldiers and Their Employment in the Assyrian Army', in *Ethnicity in Ancient Mesopotamia*, ed. W. H. van Soldt (Leiden, 2005), pp. 222–44

—, 'Neo-Assyrian State Seals: An Allegory of Power', *State Archives of Assyria Bulletin*, XVIII (2011), pp. 215–43

—, 'Outcomes of Battle: Triumphal Celebrations in Assyria', in *Rituals of Triumph in the Mediterranean World*, ed. A. Spalinger and J. Armstrong (Leiden, 2013), pp. 75–94

—, 'Images of Assyrian Sieges: What They Show, What We Know, What We Can Say', in *Brill's Companion to Sieges in the Ancient Mediterranean*, ed. J. Armstrong and M. Trundle (Leiden and Boston, MA, 2019), pp. 53–68

Novotny, Jamie, and Joshua Jeffers, *The Royal Inscriptions of Ashurbanipal (668–631 BC), Assur-etal-ilani (630–627 BC), and Sin-sarra-iskun (626–612 BC), Kings of Assyria*, Part I (University Park, PA, 2018)

Oates, Joan, and David Oates, *Nimrud: An Assyrian Imperial City Revealed* (London, 2001)

Oppenheim, A. Leo, 'The City of Assur in 714 B.C.', *Journal of Near Eastern Studies*, XIX/2 (1960), pp. 133–47

Parpola, Simo, *The Correspondence of Sargon II*, Part I: *Letters from Assyria and the West* (Helsinki, 1987)

—, *Assyrian Royal Rituals and Cultic Texts: Letters from Assyrian and Babylonian Scholars* (Helsinki, 1993)

—, 'Cuneiform Texts from Ziyaret Tepe (Tushan), 2002–2003', *State Archives of Assyria Bulletin*, XVII (2008), pp. 1–113

—, *Assyrian Royal Rituals and Cultic Texts* (Helsinki, 2017)

Parpola, Simo, and Kazuko Watanabe, *Neo-Assyrian Treaties and Loyalty Oaths* (Helsinki, 1988)

Pickworth, Diana, 'Excavations at Nineveh: The Halzi Gate', *Iraq*, LXVII/1 (2005), pp. 295–316

Podany, Amanda H., *Brotherhood of Kings* (New York, 2010)

Pongratz-Leisten, Beate, *Religion and Ideology in Assyria* (Munich and Boston, MA, 2015)

Portuese, Ludovico, *Life at Court: Ideology and Audience in the Late Assyrian Palace* (Münster, 2020)

Potts, Daniel T., *The Archaeology of Elam* (Cambridge, 2016)

Radner, Karen, 'The Trials of Esarhaddon: The Conspiracy of 670 BC', *ISIMU*, VI (2003), pp. 165–83

—, 'The Delegation of Power: Neo-Assyrian Bureau Seals', in *L'archive des fortifications de Persépolis: État des questions et perspectives de recherches*, ed. P. Briant et al. (Paris, 2008), pp. 481–515

—, 'The Assur–Nineveh–Arbela Triangle: Central Assyria in the Neo-Assyrian Period', in *Between the Cultures: The Central Tigris Region in Mesopotamia from the 3rd to the 1st Millennium* BC, ed. P. Miglus and S. Mühl (Heidelberg, 2011), pp. 321–9
—, 'Royal Decision-Making: Kings, Magnates and Scholars', in *The Oxford Handbook of Cuneiform Culture*, ed. K. Radner and E. Robson (Oxford, 2011), pp. 358–79
—, 'After Eltekeh: Royal Hostages from Egypt at the Assyrian Court', in *Stories of Long Ago: Festschrift für Michael D. Roaf*, ed. H. Baker, K. Kaniuth and A. Otton (Münster, 2012), pp. 471–9
—, 'Assyria and the Medes', in *The Oxford Handbook of Ancient Iran*, ed. D. T. Potts (Oxford, 2013), pp. 442–56
—, 'An Imperial Communication Network: The State Correspondence of the Neo-Assyrian Empire', in *State Correspondence in the Ancient World: From New Kingdom Egypt to the Roman Empire*, ed. K. Radner (Oxford, 2014), pp. 64–93
—, 'High Visibility Punishment and Deterrent: Impalement in Assyrian Warfare and Legal Practice', *Zeitschrift für Altorientalische und Biblische Rechtsgeschichte*, XXI (2015), pp. 103–28
—, 'Revolts in the Assyrian Empire: Succession Wars, Rebellions against a False King and Independence Movements', in *Revolt and Resistance in the Ancient Classical World and the Near East: In the Crucible of Empire*, ed. J. J. Collins and J. G. Manning (Leiden, 2016), pp. 39–54
—, 'Assur's "Second Temple Period": The Restoration of the Cult of Aššur, *c.* 538 BC', in *Herrschaftslegitimation in vorderorientalischen Reichen der Eisenzeit*, ed. C. Levin and R. Müller (Tübingen, 2017), pp. 77–96
—, 'Assyrian Imperial Power and How to Oppose It', The Institute for the Study of Ancient Cultures, University of Chicago, lecture delivered 1 May 2019, www.youtube.com
—, 'Last Emperor or Crown Prince Forever? Aššur-uballiṭ II of Assyria According to Archival Sources', *State Archives of Assyria Studies*, XXVIII (2019), pp. 135–42
—, 'Mass Deportation: The Assyrian Resettlement Policy', *Assyrian Empire Builders*, University College London, 2021, http://oracc.museum.upenn.edu
—, 'Running the Empire: Assyrian Governance', *Assyrian Empire Builders*, University College London, 2021, http://oracc.museum.upenn.edu.
Reade, Julian E., 'Das Kultrelief aus Assur: Glas, Ziegen, Zapfen und Wasser', *Mitteilungen der Deutschen Orient-Gesellschaft zu Berlin*, CXXXII (2000), pp. 105–12
—, 'The Ishtar Temple at Nineveh', *Iraq*, LXVII/1 (2005), pp. 347–90
Rich, Claudius James, *Narrative of a Residence in Kurdistan and on the Site of Ancient Nineveh*, vol. II (London, 1836)
Roaf, Michael, 'Cyaxares in Assyria', *NABU*, 4 (2021), pp. 277–9
Robson, Eleanor, *Ancient Knowledge Networks: A Social Geography of Cuneiform Scholarship in First-Millennium Assyria and Babylonia* (London, 2019)

Russell, John M., *From Nineveh to New York: The Strange Story of the Assyrian Reliefs in the Metropolitan Museum and the Hidden Masterpiece at Canford School* (New Haven, CT, and London, 1997)
—, 'Assyrian Cities and Architecture', in *A Companion to Assyria*, ed. E. Frahm (New Haven, CT, 2017), pp. 423–52
Saint-Laurent, Jeanne-Nicole Mellon and Kyle Smith, eds, *The History of Mar Behnam and Sarah: Martyrdom and Monasticism in Medieval Iraq* (Piscataway, NJ, 2018)
Salvesen, Alison, 'The Legacy of Babylon and Nineveh in Aramaic Sources', in *The Legacy of Mesopotamia*, ed. S. Dalley (Oxford, 1998), pp. 139–62
Simpson, St John, 'From Persepolis to Babylon and Nineveh: The Rediscovery of the Ancient Near East', in *Enlightenment: Discovering the World in the Eighteenth Century*, ed. K. Sloan and A. Burnett (London, 2003), pp. 192–201
—, 'Annihilating Assyria', in *In Context: The Reade Festschrift*, ed. I. L. Finkel and St J. Simpson (Oxford, 2020), pp. 141–68
Southgate, Horatio, *Narrative of a Visit to the Syrian Jacobite Church of Mesopotamia; with Statements and Reflections upon the Present State of Christianity in Turkey, and the Character and Prospects of the Eastern Churches* (New York, 1844)
Spar, Ira, *Cuneiform Texts in the Metropolitan Museum of Art*, vol. I: *Tablets, Cones, and Bricks of the Third and Second Millennium BC* (New York, 1988)
Starr, Ivan, *Queries to the Sungod: Divination and Politics in Sargonid Assyria* (Helsinki, 1990)
Stein, Diana L., 'A Reappraisal of the "Sauštatar Letter" from Nuzi', *Zeitschrift für Assyriologie*, LXXXIV/1 (1989), pp. 11–37
Steiner, Richard C., and Charles F. Nims. 'Ashurbanipal and Shamash-shum-ukin: A Tale of Two Brothers from the Aramaic Text in Demotic Script. Part 1', *Revue biblique (1946–)*, XCII/1 (1985), pp. 60–81
Steinkeller, Piotr, 'Tiš-atal's Visit to Nippur', *NABU*, 15 (2007), p. 108
Svärd, Saana, *Women and Power in Neo-Assyrian Palaces* (Helsinki, 2015)
Tadmor, Hayim and Shigeo Yamada, *The Royal Inscriptions of Tiglath-pileser III (744–727 BC) and Shalmaneser V (726–722 BC), Kings of Assyria* (Winona Lake, IN, 2011)
Taylor, Jonathan, 'Knowledge: The Key to Assyrian Power', in *I Am Ashurbanipal: King of the World, King of Assyria*, ed. G. Brereton (London, 2018), pp. 88–97
Thavapalan, Shiyanthi, 'A World in Color: Polychromy of Assyrian Sculpture', in *Ancient Mesopotamia Speaks: Highlights of the Yale Babylonian Collection*, ed. A. Lassen, E. Frahm and K. Wagensonner (New Haven, CT, 2019), pp. 193–200
Valk, Jonathan, 'The Origins of the Assyrian King List', *Journal of Ancient Near Eastern History*, VI/1 (2019), pp. 1–17
Van de Mieroop, Marc, *Philosophy Before the Greeks: The Pursuit of Truth in Ancient Babylonia* (Princeton, NJ, 2016)
Veenhof, Klaas R., 'The Old Assyrian Period (20th–18th Century BCE)', in *A Companion to Assyria*, ed. E. Frahm (New Haven, CT, 2017), pp. 57–79

Weissert, Elnathan, 'Royal Hunt and Royal Triumph in a Prism Fragment of Assurbanipal', in ASSYRIA *1995: Proceedings of the 10th Anniversary Symposium of the Neo-Assyrian Text Corpus Project, Helsinki, September 7–11*, ed. S. Parpola and R. M. Whiting (Helsinki, 1995), pp. 339–58

Wengow, David, '"The Changing Face of Clay": Continuity and Change in the Transition from Village to Urban Life in the Near East', *Antiquity*, LXXII/278 (1998), pp. 783–95

Wiggermann, F.A.M., 'Lamaštu, Daughter of Anu: A Profile', in *Birth in Babylonia and the Bible: Its Mediterranean Setting*, ed. M. Stol (Groningen, 2000), pp. 217–52

ACKNOWLEDGEMENTS

This book draws on the scholarship and encouragement of many individuals but I am especially indebted to John Curtis, Julian Reade, Irene Winter, Zainab Bahrani, Eleanor Robson, Karen Radner and my Oxford students. I am grateful to Dave Watkins for inviting me to submit a proposal on the Assyrians and to Michael Leaman and Amy Salter at Reaktion Books for skilfully guiding the book to completion.

PHOTO ACKNOWLEDGEMENTS

The author and publishers wish to express their thanks to the sources listed below for illustrative material and/or permission to reproduce it. Some locations of artworks are also given below, in the interest of brevity:

Ashmolean Museum, University of Oxford: pp. 99, 129, 132; British Institute for the Study of Iraq: pp. 27, 34, 59, 83; British Institute for the Study of Iraq/State Board of Antiquities and Heritage: pp. 90, 91; © The Trustees of the British Museum: pp. 66, 78, 94, 98, 119 and cover (photograph by Joanna Fernandes), 152, 157, 160, 166; Paul Collins: pp. 75, 106, 107; Metropolitan Museum of Art, New York: pp. 18 (gift of John D. Rockefeller Jr, 1933/public domain), 41 left and right (gift of Mr. and Mrs. J. J. Klejman, 1966/public domain), 48 (Rogers Fund, 1924/public domain), 50 (gift of J. Pierpont Morgan, 1911/public domain), 63 (gift of John D. Rockefeller Jr, 1932/public domain), 68 (gift of John D. Rockefeller Jr, 1932/public domain), 69 (gift of John D. Rockefeller Jr, 1932/public domain), 70–71 (Rogers Fund, 1959/public domain); Miia Ranta: p. 86; from Anton Moortgat, *The Art of Ancient Mesopotamia* (London and New York, 1969), pl. 204: p. 45; John Murray Publishers, 1853: p. 10 (public domain); Musée du Louvre, Paris: p. 14 (public domain); The Victorian Web (https://victorianweb.org): p. 19 (photograph by George P. Landow).

Creative Commons: pp. 22, 31, 36, 62, 102, 125 top and bottom, 145, 174 (Osama Shukir Muhammed Amin FRCP (Glasg)/CC BY-SA 4.0 International); 26 (Blank Map by Fulvio314/ CC BY-SA 3.0 Unported/Detail by Paul Collins); 52 (Hermann Junghans/ CC BY-SA 3.0 Unported); 93 (Jastrow (2006)/public domain); 110 (Zunkir/ CC BY-SA 4.0 International); 116–17 (Steven G. Johnson/ CC BY-SA 3.0 Unported); 124 (Paul Hudson from United Kingdom/CC BY 2.0 Generic); 138 (Internet Archive Book Images/No known copyright restrictions); 144 (Rama/ CC BY-SA 3.0 FR); 148, 156, 161 (Carole Raddato from Frankfurt, Germany/ CC BY-SA 2.0 Generic); 162–3 (Allan Gluck/ CC BY 4.0 International); 176 (Gabriel Tranchand/public domain).

INDEX

Page numbers in *italics* refer to illustrations